THE TEACHER TOOLKIT
GUIDE TO
QUESTIONING

PRAISE FOR THE TEACHER TOOLKIT GUIDE TO QUESTIONING

'The book is packed with actionable tips, techniques, and examples that can be easily implemented in any classroom. I believe that this book is an essential resource for any educator who wants to create a more engaging and effective learning environment.'

Kaye MacIver, Regional Director of Learning, Vietnam and Thailand, International Schools Partnership Limited

'Ross cuts through the noise of an extensive evidence base to provide yet another compelling and practicable guide to one of the most powerful tools at a teacher's disposal – a must-read for any teacher.'

Dr Martin Rigby, Deputy Principal, Runshaw College

'Another excellent book from Ross. This fantastic guide to questioning is steeped in theory, giving practical and readily usable questioning techniques to ensure effective classroom practice. Questioning is the key ingredient in any classroom and this book is a key ingredient to any teacher's toolkit.'

Mrs Jane Dunnett, Deputy Headteacher, The Robert Napier School

'Regardless of experience, there are tweaks you will immediately make to your practice that will increase your ability to use questions to efficiently check for and deepen understanding. I cannot wait to plan professional development for our teachers using the "bringing it all together" section.'

Anna Chidzey, Primary Deputy Head at British International School Riyadh

'Ross has added yet another must-read for teachers to further enhance one of the most important, and most taken for granted strategies in the teacher toolkit - questioning. This book provides a concise analysis of the evidence base before taking the reader through a methodical approach to trial questioning techniques in the classroom with ease. At a time where teacher workload is ever growing, this book provides a practical approach to teacher improvement.'

Jamie Watkinson, Assistant Principal at John Leggott College

'Ross has written a go-to resource to make the process of questioning more effective and impactful. Packed with actionable practical ideas that give clear insight into the evidence underpinning questioning strategies, every chapter provides an opportunity to reflect on one's own practice. This is an essential addition to your Teaching (and Questioning) Toolkit!'

Jon Wyse, Elite Sport Manager at Loughborough College

'What will you do with the information in this book? Will you pop the book on your shelf alongside the other great books by Ross McGill? Your teaching practice will be poorer if you let this work gather dust. Underpinned by strong research and practical examples from the EYFS classroom upwards, allow (in my eyes) a master educator to help you reframe your questioning. Feeling the different vibe across my class already!'

Rosemary Arnold-Knights, supply teacher at Engage Education

'All teachers must read this book. Questioning should be a major tool in our teaching toolkit and this is full of strategies to increase both hard thinking and student engagement. Ross writes in a conversational manner which is easy to read and digest. His tried and tested approach to books means that you get an explanation of the concept, followed by examples of what it could look like in the classroom and a writing frame to help plan when you might give an idea a try. Insightful on both the use of questioning and the theories of cognitive science which provide reasoning behind each strategy.'

Maria Bateson, KS5 Science Lead, The Charter School East Dulwich

'Once again, Ross McGill has produced an informative and educational book that will be of use across the profession, covered in sticky notes and highlights along with scribbled, somewhat illegible notes in the margins, showing what a knowledgeable author he is. It's a useful tool because it collates a very large amount of research with more recent understanding and knowledge, pulling it all together in one seamless well-structured resource.'

Andrea Rason, English, Maths and ICT Teacher at The Sheffield College

'The best piece of advice I received from my teacher training was that questioning is the most important skill a teacher can employ in the classroom. This book puts questioning on the pedestal it deserves. It is rooted in evidence-based practice and showcases the multifaceted nature of the topic.'

Amy Smith, Head of A level Biology, St Christopher's C E High School, Accrington

BLOOMSBURY EDUCATION
Bloomsbury Publishing Plc
50 Bedford Square, London, WC1B 3DP, UK
29 Earlsfort Terrace, Dublin 2, Ireland

BLOOMSBURY, BLOOMSBURY EDUCATION and the Diana logo are
trademarks of Bloomsbury Publishing Plc

First published in Great Britain, 2023

This edition published in Great Britain, 2023 by Bloomsbury Publishing Plc

A catalogue record for this book is available from the British Library

ISBN: PB: 978-1-4729-8938-3 ; ePDF: 978-1-4729-8936-9;
ePub: 978-1-4729-8937-6

2 4 6 8 10 9 7 5 3 1 (paperback)

Text design by Marcus Duck Design

Printed and bound in the UK by CPI Group Ltd, CR0 4YY

To find out more about our authors and books visit www.bloomsbury.com
and sign up for our newsletters

THE TEACHER TOOLKIT
GUIDE TO
QUESTIONING

ROSS MORRISON McGILL

BLOOMSBURY EDUCATION

LONDON OXFORD NEW YORK NEW DELHI SYDNEY

CONTENTS

ACKNOWLEDGEMENTS

What if asking the right questions could unlock a world of possibilities in education? This question has been at the heart of my writing journey over the last year, which has been filled with challenges and reflections.

The saying 'behind every successful person' resonates deeply with me, emphasising the crucial role of supportive individuals in our lives. I am fortunate to have such a person in my grounded and creative wife, **Jenni**. Without her unwavering support, none of the @TeacherToolkit productions would be possible. Jenni, your contributions are invaluable, and I am forever grateful.

I extend my heartfelt appreciation to the fandabbydozy team at Bloomsbury, particularly **Emily**, who has shown remarkable patience, nudging me forward when necessary and gracefully handling the multitude of challenges I tend to create back at HQ.

Dr. Bethany Kelly, a true legend, deserves special mention for generously agreeing to write the foreword to this book. Her words offer profound insights, delivered with elegance and brevity, that will surely resonate with every reader. I am indebted to accomplished teachers **Dr. Ute Steenkamp** and **Kate Bradley FCCT** for meticulously proofreading the book and identifying any potential missteps. Your attention to detail and guidance have been invaluable.

Lastly, I would like to acknowledge my son, **Freddie**, now 12 years old, who has appeared in the acknowledgement section in all of my books. As you grow into a remarkable human being, contributing to my social media content and inspiring me daily, your name will always be featured as my source of inspiration. Each passing year, your perspective on the education system enriches my own, and I am forever grateful to the teachers who taught you. It is my hope that this book helps others learn the art of posing questions to young people like you, who are coming of age in a world where sustaining engagement can be incredibly challenging.

What questions will you ask to shape the future of education?

Scan the QR code to listen to a short welcome message I have recorded for you.

FOREWORD

Questioning is a fundamental part of our professionalism as a teacher, which is why this book is such an important resource. Questioning runs through our practice whether we are working in Early Years, engaged with a Year 5 literacy lesson, leading a Year 9 PE lesson on the pitch, delivering online GCSE revision sessions or teaching A level chemists. Educational guides often want to simplify everything, but why undersell ourselves? There are so many different questioning techniques, theories and strategies that we should enjoy that it becomes complicated. Our ability to craft and integrate questioning is a sign of our skill as an effective practitioner. Rather than leave this integration to chance, Ross McGill provides a structured tour of questioning underpinned by recognised research. Many other educational publications provide tokenistic references to the role that research can play with teaching, but Ross McGill's own studies and research in this area provide a bridge between academic exploration and everyday practice of this critical aspect of our work. In a time when it can feel that teachers are being told there is only one 'right way' to do things, this book provides debate that reassures us that we must continue to question and challenge our own practice. There is always a danger that, as with planning, the more experienced we become as practitioners, the less time is devoted to questioning, perhaps sensing this has now become intuitive. However, the longer I am in education the more I recognise that our skills, as critically reflective practitioners, can be constantly refined. Rather than questioning becoming a last-minute thought, here it is placed at the heart of the learning process with the opportunity for it to be one of the teacher's most powerful strategies for their teaching and their own development.

Starting with the basics of our intentions and approaches, Ross explores how we can hone our professional questioning skills to aid student progress. This is interwoven with the latest thinking on cognition, feedback and recall. As teachers we should embrace the complexity and thoughtfulness of our practice. As professionals we can work towards Pinter-esque levels of engagement with strategic pauses ensuring our lessons facilitate space for thinking.

This guide is suitable for teachers at the start of their professional careers so that they can grapple with ways to build upon their planning. It is, however, also an excellent choice for experienced teachers and leaders to remind them of the underpinning thinking that they have encountered through the years.

For example, wait time – one of my own favourite approaches – is explored here in relation to the significant research available on this topic, yet it is an approach that gets remembered then forgotten only to be rediscovered at various intervals. Working first with students and then educating the next generation of teachers, I have been fortunate to see how these practices make a tangible difference in the hundreds of lessons I have observed.

It is timely that Ross has also highlighted the important link between questioning, coaching, professional development and mentoring.
Our questioning, when used well, is not only going to be one of the most influential factors in the development of student attainment, but is also a skill that may uncover thoughts, feelings, issues and motivational challenges. This could be when working with your students or may well be when working with colleagues. The need for answers in this context takes on an entirely different level of meaning.

This is not simply a 'how-to' guide, but goes much further to explain the underlying reasoning, to evaluate impact and to question significance. Again, the sign of a great teacher is not just the way they deliver their lesson, but it is the how and why that lie behind the delivery. That careful selection of the best strategy at the right time is something that can take our questioning from a basic exchange to the most thoughtful development of thinking.

Throughout the text there are incredibly helpful links to relevant reading, enabling teachers to engage first-hand with the research themselves. At the same time Ross explores practical approaches that can be applied directly to your own delivery. Strategies are set in a range of different scenarios to help teachers evaluate the ways in which these may or may not work in their own context. Templates are also provided throughout, so that a wide range of resources are available for immediate use.

I'm sure there are times when I have taken on the role of the gadfly (Chapter 4) and I'm pleased that we also have Ross to be a gadfly in putting together this book. We all can be engaged in challenging the status quo and encouraging people to think critically. Questioning should be celebrated as a joyous part of our professional role and this book does just that.

Professor Bethany Kelly
Associate Professor of Professional Practice
Director of Programmes
Faculty of Education, University of Buckingham

INTRODUCTION
WHAT MAKES A GREAT QUESTION FOR THE CLASSROOM?

What is questioning? Why do we question?

As humans, we ask other people questions every day. Asking questions helps us to understand one another. Posing them allows us to gather more information and helps us to process the world around us. In our personal lives, we probably do this subconsciously, yet in the classroom, posing key questions is a conscious decision that teachers make.

One of the earliest 'historical accounts of questioning used in the education process [can be] traced back to Socrates' (Tienken et al., 2009, p.39). This historical account describes a process that involves asking questions to help reflect and think critically about the subject. The account argues that questioning 'may be the **most frequently used teacher instructional intervention**' (p. 39).

Let us begin with the most important definition of the word 'question' itself. What does it mean? Where did it originate? According to the Cambridge Dictionary, the word 'question' is defined as 'a sentence or phrase used to find out information'. Since the turn of the century, little disagreement has existed concerning the definition of questions: they are 'concerned with information seeking and stimulate some kind of mental activity or thinking' (Wilen, 1991, p. 6).

One of the first systematic reviews into questioning in the first half of the twentieth century found that teacher questions and student answers occupied approximately '80 per cent of the average school day' (Stevens, 1912, p.22). Given the period, one reference draws upon the observations of the school principal, who estimated that 'teacher activity was 85 per cent', concluding that 'the reason why our pupils gain so little in intellectual power is because our teachers do the intellectual work' (Stevens, 1912, p. 22).

Questioning is a complex linguistic tool, which helps to assess learning at various levels:

1. Functional: the particular mental or emotional capacities involved.

2. Dynamic: whether the question encourages exploration and diverse perspectives or restricts options.

3. Difficulty: Relates to the level of intricacy and the extent of the challenge presented to the student.

4. Interest: Describes the level of engagement and attentiveness sparked in the student.

5. Feasibility: Reflects the student's capability to comprehend the question effectively. (Adapted from Wilen, 1991, p.6)

Drawing from the above definitions, when teachers pose a question, that question should be designed to find information with quality. Simple open and closed questions seek to find the correct answer, yet when using more analytical and evaluative responses, teachers naturally draw out more information from students by adding in more questions for clarity. This is something that we will explore together.

Teachers' questions

As a teacher, you are likely to ask as many as 300 to 400 questions daily (Levin and Long, 1981). Simple calculations estimate that this number alone divided by five daily lessons equates to approximately 60 questions every lesson. Given that most teachers teach approximately five lessons a day across 190 days in any academic year, even if this estimate was reduced by a third, you could pose up to 19,000 questions every year. When you take a moment to digest this phenomenal figure, your thoughts may turn towards teacher training. Suppose that questioning is one of the most frequently used teacher instructional techniques. Why do we not spend more time developing the strategies during our formative years and throughout our teacher training sessions in our schools and colleges?

A literature review on questioning techniques by Buchanan-Hill (2016) aimed to discover why certain questions 'encourage deeper thinking and elicit fuller responses' (p. 1). The study suggests that 'questioning is one of the basic techniques teachers can use to stimulate thinking, learning, and class participation' (p. 2). Thankfully, the research explains the complex breadth and depth of effective questioning – quite the opposite of a 'basic technique'. The research concludes that teachers must 'involve students more actively in their own learning' (p. 10), suggesting 'that students should be taught to ask questions as well as answer them' (p. 9), strengthening the need for teachers not only to pose questions but also to teach students how to process their thinking and how to respond.

Effective teaching requires carefully planned questions, as well as the ability to respond in the moment to a wide range of scenarios. Helping all students to develop study, self-regulation and metacognition skills are just as important to the learning process as they are to the teaching process (Dunlosky et al, 2013).

As teachers, we deliberately ask students numerous questions on an hourly basis. Many of them are conversational, ad hoc and subconscious. Occasionally one or two are explicit and designed to draw out misconceptions, check for understanding, inspire or hold individual students to account. Not all questions may be effective, lead to action or to a correct response. Some of the questions that a teacher might ask could be poorly framed, mistimed or (accidentally) provocative. As a result, this can lead to dismissive and non-verbal responses or maybe aggressive behaviour, which is counterintuitive to a teacher's moral purpose. For example, if we pitch a question wrongly, it could lead a student to respond in a way that we did not intend or frame their thinking in such a way that it leads to an incorrect answer or demotivation on their part.

Whether in the conversational moment or planned on paper, question design is important to all of us if we seek to achieve the information that we hope for from posing the question in the first place. For teachers, question design is essential. For example, 'don't know' responses result from poor question design.

There are copious influences and scenarios to consider. I will discuss this wide range of circumstances throughout the book, alongside some practical techniques for teachers to use to work more consciously and efficiently. Posing questions must be explicitly taught to all teachers. Any questions that teachers consciously decide to ask (among the hundreds of other tasks they do in a classroom at any given time) can likely be better thought-through and better designed with little conscious effort. Effective questioning stems from secure subject knowledge, strong curriculum planning, effective instruction and a secure grasp of how learning happens.

How many questions do you think that I have posed throughout this entire book? (See the answer on page 157.) What makes a good or a bad question? Are both of these questions good examples? They might be good examples of good questions but context, definition and environmental influence are always important aspects to consider. However, given that you are reading a book about teaching and this is a book for teachers, leaders and coaches, we can now get a little closer to and a little better at answering some of these questions.

Why write this book?

I wanted to write this book for two reasons. Firstly, I wanted to explore how we can ask better questions in our personal lives, using various techniques to listen more effectively, hold others to account, and to support and challenge people around us – whether family and loved ones or people we meet in our day-to-day work. Through the use of effective questioning, we can unravel others' beliefs, and we can help to develop our minds, understand what our own beliefs are and process any developing concepts and ideas, as well as get to know ourselves a little better overall.

Secondly, and more importantly for this book, my aim was to provide you as a teacher with a wide range of questioning techniques so that you can learn one or two of them at a deep and meaningful level – to use techniques more explicitly to a point of automaticity. All teachers encounter some of the most popular questioning strategies during teacher training days, often from blogs or via social media videos, but rarely are you exposed to the research on effective questioning or offered walkthrough scenarios and explanations.

In this book, I want to go one step further with you to explain some of the **most popular strategies**, why and how they work, and what you can do to embed them into your practice. In doing so, your teaching will become highly effective and, as a by-product, you will have more meaningful conversations with people in your personal and working life.

The ability to ask brilliant questions not only rests with the knowledge acquisition that you possess and your ability to process information in the moment, but it also depends on the art of listening and how you respond. Context matters, so I will provide you with a wide range of scenarios to help you to understand how to utilise questions in particular situations in order to draw specific responses, whether this is in a high-challenge scenario or a relaxing situation. As a result, some examples I provide will be presented in script form, like reading the opening scene of a movie.

The research process

Keen to follow the traditions of my previous books *Just Great Teaching* and *The Teacher Toolkit Guide to Memory*, as part of the design construction to this book, I have gathered observational research from my extensive social media network of teachers to gather their views on questioning in the classroom.

At the time of writing, over 300 teachers responded, providing over 14,000 pieces of data. A good proportion of teachers reported that they don't have much confidence in the historical/research origins of effective questioning in the classroom. There were almost no areas of questioning theory which teachers reported they were very confident about. In open-ended responses to questions about their confidence, one person said, 'Through my teacher training I engaged with research, but I am unclear on how to be an effective questioner myself.' Another teacher said, 'Staff have little awareness of metacognition currently – this is being addressed, but I believe this is the fundamental knowledge required for successful questioning.'

If you would like to take part in the data collection, the research site is still open. Scan the QR code to join.

In my long life as a school leader, I soon learned that definitions are critical. In the context of questioning, specificity is essential to help draw conclusions. At its most basic definition, specificity means that we want an answer when we ask a question. When we pose a specific question, we hope that it elicits a specific answer; one that is the right answer or at least a better one than previously provided. If we ask a bad question, we can run around in circles, ask for clarification or get frustrated.

Put simply, effective questioning helps you to get the information back that you want (or need) to know. Add 30 students into the mix and you can see why asking questions is a critical day-to-day necessity for all teachers who work on their feet five or six lessons a day. The more data that a teacher can gather in the moment, the more effectively they can question. This reinforces why online assessment platforms have allowed teachers to reduce marking, evaluate student responses and then 'plug in' interventions there and then. In an edtech era, 'retrieval'-type software can make recommendations. The teacher in the classroom, who understands the context, can translate online findings and share them with students. We haven't yet reached this high level of efficiency with questioning, although there are evolving products on the market at the time of writing.

There is one problem with online software that we should consider, which is the fact that it has not yet reached the ability to replicate or match many of the solutions currently provided in our schools. Very few pieces of software consider the individual working memory/cognitive ability of the student sitting in front of them.

HOW TO USE THIS BOOK

What you'll find in each chapter

In this book, I explore what I've been learning about questioning and why I truly believe that designing and posing instructional interventions will change how you teach. My hope in this book is to show you how you can achieve this. As educators, we have important choices influencing how we can support (or hinder) the learning process. For example, what kind of question supports knowledge retention and what questioning format elicits knowledge transfer? When should teachers pause, how long for and when should teachers respond to an answer? It's not just a matter of 'what works', it's also a question of 'why and how.'

My key objective is to provide you with some initial theory and turn the content into a practical activity for you to complete as you read through the book, modelling the learning process for you as you work through the material. Each chapter is therefore divided into four key sections.

| Explainer | Practical idea | Worked example | Template |
| 1 | 2 | 3 | 4 |

1. Explainer

The first part of each chapter covers **what you need to know** about the discussed topic. We'll delve into the research on various questioning models and case studies, conducted (largely) in schools, how questions are framed, the different types of questions, and **key theories** such as **wait time** and **funnel questions**. The explainers are supported by diagrams that will promote your understanding of these concepts.

2. Practical idea

After the explainer, we'll consider a practical idea (or ideas) that turn the questioning **theory into practice**. There will be conversational scripts to demonstrate how a questioning scenario may play out in the classroom or in other real-life scenarios, step-by-step instructions for implementing the idea in the classroom, plus recommendations and suggestions for how you might be able to apply the idea to best effect in your context.

At the end of the idea, you'll find a set of **toolkit tips**, which are practical takeaways to support you when putting the idea into practice in your classroom.

3. Worked example

For each practical idea, I'll give you a **clear example** of how it might work in practice. In these sections, I aim to demonstrate how the ideas support knowledge retention by devising a series of exercises for you to complete.

4. Template

At the end of each chapter, a **blank template** is provided to help you plan how to implement the practical ideas in your classroom. Use the templates to make the idea relevant to your students and translate the concept into your context. When you're delivering the practical ideas or using the templates with your students, it's a good idea to name the technique that you are using – for example, the **ABC** questioning approach (Chapter 6) or the **question matrix** (Chapter 7). This will help your students to identify each technique and enable them to learn how to respond and understand what is expected of them.

The templates are also available online, so you can download and print them. Scan the **QR code** that relates to each chapter template on p. 155.

Bringing it all together

In the final part of the book, I will show you how you can bring all the practical ideas together to support learning across an academic year. I will suggest how you might embed the ideas in teacher training sessions so that the ideas complement and build on each other to maximise their impact on student outcomes.

What the book will cover

Question types

There are topics covering when to use various question types, the different questions that teachers can ask, the rules involved when designing questions and the importance of trial and error. You will explore questions to ask in the classroom and in other aspects of school life. For example, what do ambiguous questions look like? How do the right questions draw out beliefs, biases and attitudes? How do you choose the right types of questions – should you use open or closed questions?

Context

Is it the context of all conversations that matters? Their location, timing, who is involved and who is posing the question? Do influences play a significant role in question-response success? The importance of context is something that I will return to frequently in this book.

Practical approaches

To make this book as practical as possible, I have focused the ideas on all things teaching and learning. You will uncover the role of questioning in the classroom, lesson observations, appraisal, coaching and other aspects of school life. There are also QR codes used throughout the book, linked to useful research papers and videos.

What you will take away from this book

I believe that the ultimate question that needs addressing throughout this book, as I present a range of strategies to you, is how do you use various questions as a pedagogical technique? How do you give students time to process what has been said and how do you best seek a larger number of responses from students in any class, rather than just falling into the trap of conversations with one student?

By the time you reach the end of this book, you will learn some of the techniques that I have been using throughout my teaching career and how I apply them in my life as an academic and as an entrepreneur, making a side hustle alongside some of the largest educational organisations in the country.

Ultimately, as you read this book, context is key. This is something that I always stress in all of my work. Take your professional wisdom and translate these ideas into your context. You need to know what questions to ask and how and when to ask them. This is just as important as the question itself.

"Andragogy who?"

Many teachers are familiar with the word pedagogy. However, few know what 'andragogy' is: a theory that focuses on the best methods for teaching adults, developed by the American educator Malcolm Knowles in the 1970s. I now spend my working life standing in front of adults, teaching classroom pedagogy (the practice of teaching).

Knowles noticed that adults learn differently than children, and he identified several characteristics of adult learners. Adults are self-directed and responsible for their own learning, bring their life experiences to the learning process, are goal-oriented and relevancy-oriented, and they are more likely to be motivated by internal factors (Knowles, 1984).

Therefore, in each chapter I explain the relevance to the information I am writing and involve you in the learning process, asking lots of questions and providing templates for you to try. By setting clear objectives at the start of each chapter, you are encouraged to self-direct your learning, provide me with feedback (where needed) and use the ideas for reflection.

Remember, the key goal of effective teaching is to model your ideas to help make learning visible to students. This is no different for teachers in professional development scenarios. Please use the information in this book in your teaching practice or in a training session, as it is important to translate the ideas and connect them to real-world situations in your place of work. If you can achieve that from this book, then my work is done.

CHAPTER 1
HISTORY AND RESEARCH ON QUESTIONING: DEVELOPING WAIT TIME TO AID PROCESSING

History

Trying to unpick academic research on questioning in classrooms is quite a minefield. Many classroom case studies have looked into questioning over the last century, alongside teaching books on questioning like this one, with various teaching strategies becoming very popularised.

In this first chapter of the book, I want to provide a brief overview of everything that I have been reading and researching, before offering various ideas that teachers can use in specific contexts. Remember, in every chapter of the book, while there is a central theme with multiple ideas, you will be presented with a core idea in greater depth, a worked example and a template to try.

Early research, 'Some observations in German schools' (Judd, 1914, p.438), reports that 'questioning breaks into the recitation and is preceded by statements made by the teacher. The latter is usually the case in the lower grades... the length is forty-five minutes.' The author writes that 'sometimes the questioning comes at the end of the period, the first part having been devoted to the lecture by the teacher' (p. 438), with questions confined to the material presented, with 'no disposition on the part of a child to call in question any part of any statement' made by the teacher (p. 441). Teaching has significantly moved forward over the last 100 years.

In a monograph published in 1991, William Wilen reviews research findings related to oral questioning behaviours and teacher practices. The research examines the role of questioning within the broader context of classroom interaction, with a particular focus on recitation and discussion. The research sought to test rather than study questions and questioning as isolated behaviours or techniques; it examined questions within the broader context of classroom interaction. For example:

- how many and what kind of questions and questioning techniques were being deployed

- the pattern of interaction being developed

- the distribution of power and authority between teacher and students.

Using systematic observation and the collection of objective data, such as aspects of questions at a cognitive level, length and frequency, this research classified 'questions recorded by stenographers [someone who transcribes speech in shorthand] according to those stimulating memory and reflection, with particular emphasis on those eliciting comparisons and judgements from students' (Wilen, 1991, p. 12). The research paper offers a wealth of ideas from a particular period that can still resonate with many teachers today and suggests that the kinds of questions that teachers ask and the techniques they use generally match their teaching philosophy.

The decisions that teachers make when questioning rely on their prior subject knowledge, any understanding of their students and past experiences from working in similar situations. These experiences can become intuitive and sometimes, given the challenges of the classroom, teachers can opt for easier, ineffective techniques that do not support learning. For example, how often have you or I posed a question to the class that started with these four words: 'Can anyone tell me...?'

We know that teaching requires informed decision-making, rooted in theory and practice. How many teachers use a teaching technique we don't like that is backed by research, or vice versa – something that we do like using even if education research suggests that it is **not** helpful?

Wilen makes the following conclusions regarding teacher questioning from the available research literature (Wilen, 1991, pp. 34–5).

1

Low-level cognitive questions – defined as recalling basic information or knowledge that students have already learned – are dominant among teachers, resulting in only 50 per cent congruence between their questions and student responses.

2

Low-level questioning has a positive relationship with student achievement.

3

Teachers' questioning techniques can impact student achievement, but their influence on student attitudes towards discussion topics is inconclusive.

5

Teachers and students lack knowledge of appropriate questioning techniques for discussions.

6

Teachers can be trained to improve their questioning practices, as questioning is a complex aspect of communication.

4

Recitation is effective for teaching factual information, while discussions could be improved with more student initiative.

EXPLAINER

How can you work more slowly to elicit more thinking from students? It makes sense to slow down and give students a chance to think. The longer you wait, the better the reward.

Professor Mary Budd Rowe was an American educator and researcher best known for her research 'Wait-time and rewards as instructional variables: Their influence on language, logic and fate control' (1974). Published using a typewriter (I remember my school assignments vividly), her 34-page document summarises five years of influence of a variable called teacher 'wait time'. Her analysis of over 300 tape recordings showed the *mean* wait time to be **one second**.

Rowe writes about how 'visiting and recording examples of science instruction carried out in classrooms located in suburban, urban, rural areas, it finally became clear that while different curricula served as the vehicle of instruction, almost all of the discourse had one stable property: the pace of instruction was very fast' (1974, p. 3). Instead, the longer a teacher waits before insisting that students answer a question, the more inference and learning can be harnessed. In some respects, when teachers do this well, they should be mindful of cognitive load theory (Sweller 1988, Sweller et al., 1998) and balance instruction and processing at once in micro-moments.

In the complicated and busy classroom world, how can you 'teach slowly' to reap more benefits in the classroom? I wonder whether there is anything that we can still learn from Rowe's work from 1974. Summarising the research on 'wait time', there are nine student variables on the next page. It's worth explaining that by 'inflected responses', Rowe is referring to student responses being inflected as though a question is being asked.

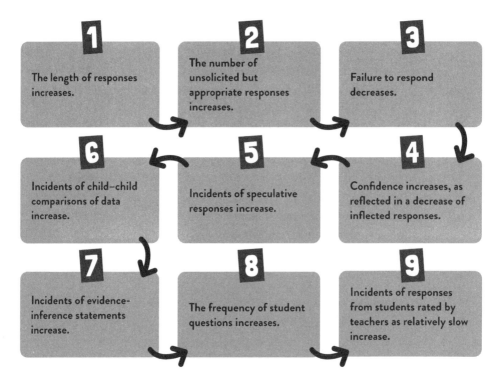

Wait time should be high and reward schedules should be reduced. If rewards are increased, it can undermine confidence and act as a distraction, with some students being rewarded with praise for their performance, while others are fearful of taking risks, playing it safe to avoid sanction. Rowe recommends that teachers work to develop a 'think system' over time, 'free of the notion of cheating and the fear of teacher reprisal' (1974, p. 4).

In some of the recommendations for things that teachers should avoid, Rowe suggests that teachers should not repeat portions of what students say or respond with 'Yes, but...' to signal a rejection of an idea; instead, teachers should ask students to think without providing either a pause or cue, plus provide evaluative comments such as 'fine', 'good work' or 'OK'. Put simply, the teacher must frame the conditions when posing questions and teach students how to wait, when they should think hard and how they should respond.

To do this well takes many years of practice. Many questioning strategies can help teachers to do this on their feet, developing a range of question types to hold students to account for their learning. Examples include pose, pause, pounce, bounce (see later in this chapter), cold calling (see Chapter 3), and no opt out (also Chapter 1). These are some of the most popular ideas that I will reference throughout this book, alongside many other techniques with which you may not be familiar by name but certainly will be through experience.

The 'wait' or 'pause' is a key phase in any process that you use. When teachers ask students questions, Rowe's research discovered that, typically, teachers waited less than one second for a student's response. Further, after a student stops speaking, teachers react or respond with another question in less than one second. The concepts of Wait Time 1 (pausing after asking a question) and Wait Time 2 (pausing after a student responds) are both discussed in her research.

In another research paper, 'Mary Budd Rowe: A storyteller of science', Bianchini (2008) explores how the 'science' of education is used to inspire professional development and innovative curriculum materials to help teachers to develop 'inquiry' in the classroom. A wonderful story from this paper is offered about Rowe, working on a problem during a flight, being asked by a boy if she would find answers in a book or from her teacher.

'No book has an answer to the problems I'm working on,' Rowe said. 'It's up to me to find the answers.'

The boy asked again, 'Will your teacher give you the correct answers... or tell you if you are right?'

Rowe replied with another 'No, I'm afraid not', before the boy sympathetically sighed, 'Some teachers are like that you know.'

Rowe's work highlights the fact that our young people often want right or wrong answers, without going beyond the facts to understand meaning that others might pass on to us. When a student asks a teacher a question, an effective technique to deploy is to reply to them and begin the process of 'story-making together' (Rowe, 1995, pp. 178–181).

Taking a brief look over historical research on effective questioning, it is clear that teaching was once a one-way product, but changes over recent decades mean that today researchers suggest that more effective teaching and learning happen when a two-way questioning process is initiated. The message? Create an inquiry culture in your classroom, teaching students how to listen and answer to questions, before responding with questions of their own to generate healthy, classroom discussions.

PRACTICAL IDEAS

Impact on students

To determine what impact teacher questioning had on students, Rowe documented the astonishing speed at which teacher and student exchanges took place. 'I fed the sound from the tapes into a servo-chart plotter...' (Rowe, 1986, p. 44), which plots the speech patterns and pauses. She made the following observations:

1. Wait time: The accumulation of pauses after student utterances before the teacher spoke again in most recordings averaged 0.9 seconds!

2. Quick reactions by teachers appeared to cut off student elaboration.

In this section, I have selected pose, pause, pounce, bounce as a practical idea to demonstrate a technique that teachers could use for immediate impact.

Recommendations

Rowe writes, 'in their eagerness to elicit responses from students, teachers often develop verbal patterns that make the achievement of Wait Time 2 unnecessarily difficult' (Rowe, 1986, p.46). Most, if not all, teachers will recognise this, particularly under observation. Rowe recommends that teachers who 'stabilize longer wait time patterns' can reap the following three benefits in class:

1. Teachers' responses exhibit greater flexibility. This is indicated by fewer discourse errors and greater continuity in developing ideas.

2. The number and type of questions asked by teachers change.

3. Expectations for the performance of certain students seem to improve. (Rowe, 1986, p.45)

Suggestions for teachers

Simple fixes for teachers could include responding to students with some of the following scripts:

- Yes, and...

- Tell me why you think this...

- What else?

- Explain to me how...

If we factor in a wide range of learning needs, this simple classroom strategy becomes more nuanced and requires many more conditions to succeed – for example, effective behaviour management, subject knowledge and personal confidence. The overall aim is for teachers to learn how best to frame a question, create the response conditions and work hard to delay any form of response to help push the thinking forward.

Unfortunately, it is difficult for many people to get average wait times up to three seconds or longer. However, we must try if we wish to reduce cognitive load and increase a degree of self-regulation in our students. Let's unpick a few ideas and recommendations from some of the research discussed so far.

Pose, pause, pounce, bounce

'Pose, pause, pounce, bounce' (or PPPB) is a brilliant questioning strategy that I have used for 15 years.

Have a read of my Guardian article 'How to move your lessons from good to outstanding' to learn more about the PPPB technique.

It is a simple yet sophisticated way to check for understanding in class and support adaptive teaching and differentiation, as well as to help to develop self-regulation and metacognition. It also encourages teachers to take risks and vary their questioning techniques. Here's how it works:

1. Pose

Explain to the class the approach that you are about to take and insist that students do not raise their hands to answer the question. Pose a question or series of questions, ensuring that you ask the students to remain reflective. Following Rowe's research recommendations, the optimum time to give students to think about what has just been asked is approximately three to five seconds.

2. Pause

This is the hard part. Pause for as long as possible before you ask anyone to answer. Ask the class to think. If students are captivated and engaged, push the boundaries and try holding the silence for a little while longer. At this stage, teachers should ask students to write something down or discuss their answer with a peer (see 'Think, pair, share', p. 28). This makes the process more concrete and provides the opportunity for students to retrieve something during the encoding (turning thoughts into communication) phase of learning. As a teacher, it is important that you seek evidence that your students are thinking about your question.

3. Pounce

Select one student for an answer. Insist that the answer comes from Student A directly, without interruption from others. It is essential that teachers plan which students they are going to ask before speaking to the class. There are several methods recommended here to avoid guesswork – for example, random name selectors found online or labelled 'lolly sticks in a jar' or whatever the teacher has to hand.

In addition to asking just one student to answer, there is the option to insist that the whole class writes down the answer on a mini white board (see Chapter 2). In some cases we can ask all students to show the teacher their response, but in a discussion scenario follow the rest of this methodology.

The teacher asks Student A to respond. Here, it's essential for the teacher to wait even longer. Remember Rowe's research recommendations? Teachers are too keen to move on or reply with 'Yes' or 'No' to student responses. Ideally, we should work hard to refrain from speaking and instead provide another period of silence. Here, a teacher is also likely to use non-verbal facial cues to support the learning process and manage classroom dynamics and relationships. While on paper it's easy to recommend 'pausing' a little more, we know that it's far from easy to wait in the classroom when around 30 students are itching to be selected to answer, or blurt out(!) the solution without being selected. Whatever happens, all teachers should aim to quash any comments or noises from the class before moving on. It's magic when you can hear, see and feel a captivated learning audience. We've all experienced it. It's important to wait for an answer, provide support (or call on peers to help) and pause your response. If it's clear that no answer is on its way, you'll need to move to someone else, but go back to this student to hold them to account. If Student A does manage to answer, then...

4. Bounce

Immediately ask another student for their opinion of Student A's answer and make sure that they explain their reasoning. This can be developed by asking a third student for their opinion, irrespective of whether the original answer is correct or not. Using this technique helps students to self-regulate their thinking and develop a range of metacognitive functions during the process. When unpacked, the teacher can help students to understand the various decisions and thought processes that they may have encountered during the questioning process – for example, helping students to understand knowledge of themselves or of the task (or question) to hand, and how best to solve the problem. This is how we help to teach metacognition.

No opt out

Almost a decade ago, when I was developing a teaching and learning policy (later published in *Mark. Plan. Teach.*, 2017), part of the extensive action research conducted by myself and colleagues was to access all the emerging research, education books and teaching materials at the time. One such book was *Teach like a Champion* by Doug Lemov (2010). Lemov systematically gathered 49 teaching techniques to 'help eliminate the gap between the achievement levels of poor privileged students' (p. xv). Inside the wide range of ideas was a technique called 'no opt out', which has been fundamental in addressing the 'don't know' responses to some of the scenarios I have described previously.

'No opt out' is a technique that can be used anywhere to hold all students to account for their learning. As Lemov writes in his first edition of *Teach Like A Champion* (2010), the strategy 'involves going back to a student who was at first unable or unwilling to provide an answer to a question', (p. 8) and either asking them to repeat the correct answer after another student in the class has provided it or, when returning to them, the teacher asks them to summarise their first answer based on what they have just heard. In essence, it's an opportunity to **say the answer again, but better** this time. Here's an example:

Let's assume that you are working with an engineering class on the topic of non-ferrous metals.

1. You ask Ross to name a non-ferrous metal and explain what makes it different to ferrous metal. Ross stares blankly and replies with, 'I don't know.'

2. As the teacher, you then move onto another student and ask the same question again. This time, you hear the correct answer and explanation.

3. Quickly, you return back to Ross and use the 'no opt out' strategy, saying, 'Ross, now give me an example of a non-ferrous metal and what makes it different to ferrous metals.'

4. This repetition ensures that Ross has no option but to try, as you have eliminated almost all risk of failure. Instead, repeating what we have just heard in class makes it easier for Ross to succeed, simply by reinstating his peer's example.

Wait time

Returning to Mary Budd Rowe's seminal research (1972), she concludes with these recommendations to improve question effectiveness:

1
Allow for a pause of three seconds (or more) between a teacher's question and an answer. It's essential that teachers give students time to process what has been said.

2
Avoid rapid-fire questioning, particularly with low-level questions based on recall. Increasing anxiety can reduce retrieval strength.

3
Give students time to think and process their answers. Adding in additional time between processing what has been said and formulating a response is just as important.

5
Encourage students to be active and engaged learners by inviting them to answer questions. This helps to build a culture of trust, risk-taking and collegiality (see Chapter 7 for further information on developing questioning culture).

4
Avoid providing answers immediately after a student responds. Responding immediately can discourage further discussion. Instead, respond with 'Why?' or 'Can you explain to me how (pause), Ross?' This simple response helps to develop metacognitive skills.

It's always worth paraphrasing what students have said. This allows a teacher to provide a consensus view, add specific details and ensure that all students have heard the correct information. Using Rowe's recommendations today, teachers can continue to improve their effectiveness and foster a highly efficient classroom environment.

TOOLKIT TIPS

1. Pause for at least three seconds after posing a question, to give students time to think.

2. Pause again after a response – avoid the temptation to repeat what they've said or jump in with a 'Yes, but...'

3. 'Bounce' the response back to another student for their opinion – this helps to develop metacognition and self-regulation.

4. Go back to students who've been unable to answer correctly and give them a chance to get it right by repeating or summarising the correct answer after hearing it from someone else.

WORKED EXAMPLE

Using what we know from research and the history of questioning in the classroom, here is a worked example of a teacher and student in dialogue in a design and technology classroom. The class has just completed a retrieval practice quiz on thermosetting plastics and their uses. They are a mixed-ability group of 30 students, aged 12 years old. They have spent the last 12 weeks completing a plastics project, exploring the benefits of thermosetting plastic products and the downsides of the material from a sustainability perspective.

Teacher: 'OK, hands down, thinking first, no calling out.' *(The teacher resets the behaviour and attention conditions for the class.)*

Teacher: *(Pauses three seconds or more and poses the following question very slowly.)* 'What are thermosetting plastics?' *(Waits another three seconds.)*

Teacher: 'Ross...' *(Gestures non-verbally to the student to respond.)*

Student: 'Thermosetting plastics become permanently rigid and fixed when heated.'

Teacher: *(Pauses three seconds or more before giving any clues or signals.)* 'A reminder, everyone. I'll pose the question. I'll ask all of you to think of an answer, then I'll select someone to reply.' *(Short pause.)*

Teacher: 'Could you give me an example of a thermosetting plastic that is hard and rigid?' *(Pauses three seconds or more.)*

Teacher: 'Fatima...'

Student: 'One example of a thermosetting plastic that is hard and rigid is polyurethane.'

Teacher: *(Pauses three seconds or more.)* 'Interesting choice Fatima. *What* kind of properties do thermosetting plastics have?' *(Pauses three seconds or more.)* 'Fatima...' *(Returning to the same student ensures that nobody switches off.)*

Student: 'Thermosetting plastics are strong, durable and resistant to heat and chemicals.'

Teacher: *(Pauses three seconds or more.)* 'What are some of the applications of thermosetting plastics?' *(Pauses three seconds or more.)* 'Ross, give me one example.'

Student: 'Thermosetting plastics are used in a variety of applications, such as coatings, adhesives and electrical insulation.'

TEMPLATE

Pose, pause, pounce, bounce

Step	Teacher Actions / Description	Student Selection / Process
1. Pose	Ask a question	
2. Pause	Wait for a response	
3. Pounce	Select a student to answer	
4. Bounce	Ask another student to comment on the response	

Wait Time

Teacher:	Okay class, today we're going to be talking about the properties of matter. Can anyone give me an example of a physical property of matter?
Student A:	Density!
Teacher:	Great job, Student A. Can you explain to the class what density is?
Student A:	Density is the amount of mass per unit volume of a substance.
Teacher:	Excellent. Now, Student B, can you give me an example of a chemical property of matter?
Student B:	Um, I don't know.
Teacher:	Okay, let's see if someone else can help us out. Student C, can you give me an example of a chemical property of matter?
Student C:	How about reactivity with water?
Teacher:	Perfect. Now, Student B, I'm going to use the 'No Opt Out' technique and ask you to summarise what Student C just said. What is an example of a chemical property of matter?
Student B:	Reactivity with water.
Teacher:	Great job, Student B! See how easy that was? We're all here to learn together and sometimes we need a little help from our peers to fully understand a concept.

For further information on how to use No Opt Out, scan the QR code and watch the video example.

CHAPTER 2
DEVELOPING CONCRETE RESPONSES (QUESTIONING IN THE PRIMARY CLASSROOM)

Questioning in an Early Years and primary context

In this chapter, I will explore **retrieval practice** (by questioning) and will share what primary teachers should consider when working with **younger students**. Retrieval practice is the process of actively trying to recall information using working memory. This can be done through activities such as quizzes, tests, flashcards and other 'revision'-like activities. This type of practice helps to strengthen memory and improves recall.

Put simply, when a teacher poses a question, this is a methodology to help students to retrieve information. From a cognitive science perspective, retrieval derives from the French fifteenth-century word *retrouver* – to return (or regain), with *trouver* meaning 'to find' and *re* meaning to 'recover' or 'revisit'. At the retrieval stage, cognitive scientists recommend a student must write it down or say it out loud: you are aiming to **pull information out** of students' heads!

In a paper published by the University of Manchester and The Ogden Trust (Bianchi et al., 2021), researchers explored ten key issues with children's learning in primary science in England. They found that teacher questioning during plenaries is 'closed and focused on recall' (p. 16). This is one of the poorer questioning techniques that a teacher can use, because it relies on learning being implicit and not explicit. From observations on assessment practice, they found that 'learning outcomes or success criteria are unclear and often so broad that it is impossible to know if the lesson or the child has been successful' (p. 16). Other issues identified in the research included challenge, teacher talk and fun science activities, all of which failed to deepen or develop learning. These findings could be alarming for teachers!

More recently, Ofsted, England's Office for Standards in Education (aka Grim Reaper), published a subject report in science, 'Finding the optimum' (2023), which highlighted similar issues to The Ogden Trust report.

'In some lessons, teachers were expected to teach too *much content* at once. This resulted in the teaching moving on before there had been time for all pupils to consolidate their knowledge, get feedback and act on it. This often occurred when a teacher's focus was on keeping pace with curriculum plans or making sure that all content had been covered before an assessment.' (para. 101)

Ofsted (Grim Reaper) also noted that 'teachers often use well-structured enquiry questions to focus an activity on a particular aspect of the curriculum' (para. 36). Teacher effectiveness was underpinned by strong subject knowledge, with students benefiting from time to discuss ideas, answer questions and practise using the knowledge. Where good practice is referenced, 'teachers' explanations and questioning build incrementally from students' prior knowledge, drawing together related knowledge from different areas of the curriculum' (para. 86). The report confirmed that questioning was the most common way in which teachers ascertained 'what their pupils knew', checking for misconceptions (which is 'rarely done') or using mini whiteboards effectively 'to reveal what everyone is thinking' (para. 104).

Insufficient checking of understanding leads to a wrong assumption on the part of the teacher (Ofsted, 2023). The result? Specific gaps in students' knowledge will emerge, and possibly embed, before they reach the end of the topic. A key question worth asking (which I will return to in the 'worked example' section of this chapter – see p. 28) is 'What techniques could a teacher build into their lesson to regularly check for misconceptions?', without it leading students to shy away from frequently getting things wrong/right, exposing working memory, or causing retrieval-induced forgetting or the phenomenon in which remembering causes the forgetting of other information.

Are there any downsides to retrieval practice? Retrieving memories can also open a window to errors when erroneous information is retrieved or when new information is encoded during retrieval.

Read more on memory retrieval, by scanning the QR code

EXPLAINER

Encode-store-retrieve is a cognitive science approach to understanding how we learn and remember information. It suggests that there are three stages involved in the process of learning and memory: encoding, storage, and retrieval. This is something I believe all teachers should know, and is something I'm sharing during my teacher training travels. I discover that very few teachers can articulate this, so together, we all need to change this.

1. **Encoding:** This is the process of taking in information and converting it into a form that can be stored in the brain. Encoding can involve various strategies, such as repetition, elaboration and organisation, and it is influenced by factors like attention, motivation and prior knowledge.

2. **Storage:** This refers to the retention of information over time. Once information has been encoded, it is stored in the brain, where it can be retrieved at a later time. The storage of information can be affected by factors such as the amount of attention paid to the information, the emotional significance of the information and the level of processing involved in encoding.

3. **Retrieval:** This is the process of accessing stored information when it is needed. Retrieval can be influenced by a variety of factors, such as the similarity between the encoding and retrieval contexts, the strength of the memory trace and the presence of cues that can trigger memory recall.

Overall, the encode-store-retrieve approach suggests that effective learning and memory involve not only the initial acquisition of information but also the storage and retrieval of that information over time. By understanding these three stages of the process, teachers can develop strategies to enhance learning and memory performance.

Retrieval practice in primary schools

There is little research on retrieval practice (questioning) conducted in primary schools. In this section, we explore **procedural**, **convergent** and **divergent questions** and how they can be implemented in classrooms. In the practical idea section of this chapter, while using think-pair-share-show me (with mini whiteboards) and whole-class feedback methods can be adopted in most classrooms, I will zoom in on using these questioning strategies (for retrieval) in a primary school context.

In a literature review, 'Teachers' questioning in classroom interaction towards students' learning process in an EFL classroom' (Izzati and Wahyuni, 2021), the researchers provide an overview of some important strategies:

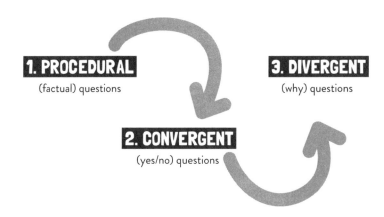

1. PROCEDURAL (factual) questions

2. CONVERGENT (yes/no) questions

3. DIVERGENT (why) questions

Procedural questions help to develop interaction between the teacher and the students – useful for when the teacher wants to check for understanding. They most often feature during classroom management and procedural-type phases of the lesson. For example, how are you today? Do you have any questions? Do you have a pencil? Fact-based answers seek to retrieve right or wrong answers – not necessarily developing knowledge transfer, but hopefully strengthening knowledge retention. Teachers use these types of questions for a large proportion of the day. Sixty-six per cent of the teachers whom I surveyed in my research for this book suggested that they found 'influences' on the questions that they asked and the techniques that they deployed as their **number one challenge** (see the graph on the next page for a breakdown of how teachers rated their biggest challenges).

WHICH ASPECTS OF WORK DO YOU FIND A CURRENT CHALLENGE?

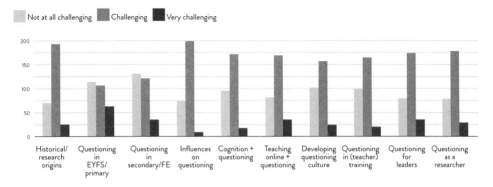

Convergent questions are designed to engage students in learning, requiring the correct answer through retrieval. For example, 'Does King Charles III's head face to the left-hand side on a £1 coin?' These types of questions can draw upon prior knowledge (knowledge retention), but teachers can then use this to help take the information one step further by asking 'Why?' or 'Explain to me how you've reached this conclusion'; this helps to develop metacognition, reinforcing the study skills of self-explanation and elaboration. Rather than 'Does King Charles III's head face to the left?', the teacher could ask 'Why does King Charles III's head face to the left-hand side on a £1 coin?' Adding the 'why' before the original question totally changes the expectations. Although there is a place for procedural and convergent questions, adding the 'why' makes a straightforward question become a convergent question. At this point, teachers working with younger children should think carefully about when they might introduce these decisions when designing questions.

Divergent questions do not have a specific answer and may have many explanations. Asking students to analyse, synthesise or evaluate topics is often a very useful strategy for teachers to deploy at the start and end of a particular curriculum. From the outset, it allows the teacher to understand what the students already know. Again, this is a challenge for teachers working with younger students, who are developing their cognitive functions in the earlier years of schooling.

In a short paper, 'Open thinking, closed questioning: Two kinds of open and closed question' (2015), Peter Worley provides a distinction between two kinds of open and closed questions. Worley offers grammatical and conceptual examples, with explanations of how and why they are important. See the QR code in the Further Reading section on p. 147 to see further examples. One example includes 'Do you like Marmite?', which is a semantically incomplete, conceptually closed question. Instead, if a teacher were to ask, 'Is it possible to be wrong about what you like?', which is a grammatically closed, conceptually open question, it is more likely to generate an interesting discussion. This subtle difference helps teachers to move students away from closed 'yes or no' responses.

The paper reminds teachers of how and why 'certain kinds of questions do or do not encourage enquiry discussion' (Worley, 2015, p. 24). Worley argues that 'grammatically open questions tend to lack focus and specificity' (p. 24) and that teachers might find themselves steering away from enquiry discussions because they lead towards managing behaviour conflicts. **The conclusion?** To use grammatically closed but conceptually open questions. The former elicit a short response, but the latter contain tension, conflict or possibilities within the question. But while these are thoroughly useful recommendations for teachers to adopt, how do you deploy them if you're working with primary, secondary or college students? This is something that we will explore in the next section.

PRACTICAL IDEAS

Procedural, convergent, divergent and evaluative questions in primary/EY context

Let's consider using procedural, convergent, divergent and also evaluative (summary) questions in a primary or Early Years classroom. In an interesting study (Ren et al., 2020), researchers sought to determine whether critical thinking (skills and disposition) could predict academic performance in primary children. The sample of 158 fourth grade students (nine-to-ten-year-olds) from a primary school in Central China used 71 multiple-choice questions covering four aspects of critical thinking skills: inductive reasoning, deductive reasoning, judging observations and credibility, and identifying assumption. One of their many conclusions was that teaching critical thinking dispositions plays a unique role in academic performance (Ren et al., 2020).

My aim here is to couple procedural, convergent, divergent and evaluative questions with two techniques that teachers could deploy in a classroom of younger students. This isn't to say that they cannot be used in classrooms with older students, but the examples provide a translation of the research that I have read on questioning and retrieval for primary teachers to consider.

Think-pair-share (show me)

Think-pair-share is a questioning strategy that teachers use to engage students. The strategy encourages students to think critically and respond with answers to a question. The process works like this:

1. The teacher poses a question to the class and allows students a few moments to think about the answer individually.

2. Afterwards, students are paired up and asked to discuss (or write down) their thoughts and ideas with each other.

3. Lastly, the teacher calls on a few pairs to share their answers with the class.

This strategy is an excellent way for teachers to assess their students' understanding en masse, providing opportunities for students to collaborate and engage in meaningful discussion. However, it's not robust enough simply using the method like this – something that I'll explain in the 'worked example' section.

Mini whiteboards and whole-class feedback

One of the greatest challenges for teachers is constantly dealing with the written marking burden – responding to students' work, making corrections, offering feedback tips and leaving written comments in books. For some teachers, this can take hours to achieve every week just to keep up! Whole-class feedback flips this assumption on its head, with teachers using assessment techniques such as think-pair-share to facilitate assessment or using mini whiteboards to provide feedback. This can be deployed in many forms, using scripts, annotated sheets and visual examples to allow groups of students to act on the instruction provided. It's particularly beneficial in the moment, rather than waiting for written confirmation of what to do days or weeks later. The best part? More and more school and college leaders trust their teachers to provide this as and when required, supporting the notion that curriculum evolution and decisions drive assessment, and not the other way around.

In many classrooms (sadly not all), teachers provide each student with a small mini whiteboard. In this technique, students write answers down and then, on teacher instruction, all the students display their answers to the teacher at once. The benefits of using this technique are provided below:

1. Writing down an answer allows students to work independently and at their own pace. By having their individual whiteboard, students can take their time to think through the problem and then write it down, without having to feel the pressure of competing with other students. It is worth teachers setting ground rules, instilling a quiet period for reflection and recording the answer.

2. It encourages collaborative learning. By having all the answers visible, students can see how their peers have solved the problem and can learn from one another. This process is highly complex, and do not underestimate the peer network that underlies relationships and social, emotional and mental health, as well as how working memory functions during a question-retrieval process.

3. The 'show me' process gives a teacher instant feedback. By seeing all the answers at once, teachers can easily identify areas for improvement and provide feedback to the whole class or individual students. It is worth considering how to manage this response, as it could be overwhelming for the teacher to process what is in front of them e.g. revealing answers one row at a time.

4. The process increases engagement. Having a whiteboard encourages students to actively participate in the lesson. It gives them an opportunity to apply their thinking in a temporary (wipe-off whiteboard) setting without the work being recorded permanently.

5. Using mini whiteboards enhances accountability. Each student is responsible for their whiteboard and can be held accountable for the answers that they come up with. The simple act of not writing anything down enables the teacher to very quickly establish who is thinking and who is not. It is worth considering pressure and the potential for editing in the moment as students realise they may have the wrong answer. One way to combat this is to ask students to put their heads on the table and hold whiteboards up high!

Five benefits for teachers include:

1. **Workload:** There is a quicker turnaround when using whole-class feedback, allowing the teacher to provide feedback to the entire class quickly and efficiently. This saves time and reduces the marking burden.

2. **Improved student engagement:** By providing whole-class feedback, teachers can foster a more engaging learning environment. This can help to keep students focused and motivated.

3. **Increased knowledge retention:** Whole-class feedback allows students to quickly gain a better understanding of the material and therefore potentially retain more of the information.

4. **Improved classroom discourse:** Whole-class feedback encourages students to engage in meaningful conversations with their peers. This helps to promote a more collaborative learning environment and foster relationships and a risk-taking culture.

5. **Increased time for professional development:** By reducing the amount of time spent on marking, teachers can dedicate more time to their own professional development. This can help to enhance their teaching skills and knowledge.

Plus, there are several reasons why providing whole-class feedback is more effective for students:

1. **Immediate:** Research suggests that when students receive immediate feedback, they are 'more engaged' (Shernoff et al., 2003).

2. **Improved understanding:** When commentary is provided by the teacher, rather than a written record, verbal feedback 'when applied well, has a positive impact on the engagement of all students' (Quinn and McGill, 2019, p. 29). It helps students to process information and clarify misconceptions. Of course, the challenge for all teachers is one person versus a classroom full of students asking for help!

3. **Improved knowledge retention:** By engaging in conversations with their peers, students can gain a better understanding of the material, retain more of the information and 'interact critically with the "knowledge" they come across' (Rolls and Hargreaves, 2022, p. 34).

4. **Increased student confidence:** Having the opportunity to talk it through allows teachers to engage with students' social, emotional and mental health aspects of learning, which in turn develops their confidence and understanding. In research on using whiteboards in mathematics classrooms, teachers reported 'increased student confidence and collaboration' and a shift from concerns about classroom management (Forrester et al., 2017, p.262).

TOOLKIT TIPS

1. Remember those pauses for children to think about the question, before pairing them up and asking them to discuss their answers.

2. Mini whiteboards are a great way for children to show you their answers without fear of permanence.

3. Whole-class feedback reduces the marking burden and allows for immediate assessment for the teacher and immediate feedback for the children.

WORKED EXAMPLE

Earlier in this chapter, identifying misconceptions – or at least teaching how to build strategies to identify misconceptions – is noted as a weak point in lesson design. Thus, a key question that we must ask is, **what technique should a teacher use to increase challenge** and reduce any threat or stress that may hinder retrieval, so that questioning can encourage all students to respond even if they get the answer wrong?

How effective are you at using one of the most-used teaching techniques in the world? All teachers are familiar with the pedagogical technique 'think, pair, share'. However, just using this strategy alone can lead to ineffective teaching and learning. It can also challenge working memory and lead to inaccurate evaluations of learning. Here are two scenarios explaining how you might use and introduce think, pair, share:

Scenario 1: Think, pair, share

Teacher: 'OK, Year 5s. I've got a question for you.' *(Three-second pause.)* 'Where is Mount Vesuvius?'

Student(s): *(One student immediately whispers the answer in earshot of the teacher. Another five or six students nearby raise their hands and begin to stretch their arm, hand to the ceiling, groaning and waving, calling for your attention.)*

Teacher: *(The teacher now realises that they have framed the question very poorly. The students sitting closest to the 'whispering individual' now get a sense of the correct answer (or not), and more hands start to wave and gesture.)*

Teacher: 'OK, everyone. Put your hands down; don't call out! I'm going to start again...' *(The teacher decides to move on quickly.)* 'Ross, what is the answer? Where is Mount Vesuvius?'

Student: 'Sir, is it in Italy?' *(said hopefully.)*

Teacher: 'Yes, good!' *(remarked with no delay.)*

The teacher then has a microsecond decision to make: to either ask the student for more detail or proceed with the lesson after using one student to say the answer out loud. Quite often, it's the latter. Yet teachers should switch to the former more often, by asking the student for more information. Because the teacher has not prepared students to recall, this leads to one or two individuals responding and disrupting the processing thinking of everyone else. Failing to frame 'how to respond' is *ineffective* teaching. Asking one rather than 30 students is also highly ineffective. Instead, teachers must work more efficiently and effectively.

All teachers use the think, pair, share methodology; however, we often default to the ineffective process of doing the think, pair, share demonstrated in Scenario 1.

As described in Scenario 2, the process of pausing to allow students to decode what has been said is critical. With a few small tweaks, all teachers can improve their effectiveness and the efficiency of this simple technique, framing the responses to ensure thinking is concrete.

Scenario 2: Think, pair, share, show me!

Here's think, pair, share with **'show me'** attached, as a more efficient scenario to consider when using the strategy.

Teacher: *(The teacher frames the expectations first, even before any mention of a question is suggested.)* 'OK, Year 7s. I'd like you to find a board pen to write with and your mini whiteboard. I am going to pose a question to you... but you cannot write anything down until I say. I need *(not want – a small subtle shift in language)* everyone to be ready to answer. You cannot call out. You cannot raise your hands. You must spend at least ten seconds thinking about what I've said before I stop you and then ask you to record your answer.'

(There is a long pause, and rather than asking 'Does everyone understand?', which is a cue to fall back into old habits of calling out or taking the lesson on another or repeated path, the teacher pauses before posing the key question.)

Teacher: 'Right, here is the question (*said with a short delay between each word*): Where is Mount Vesuvius? What town did it destroy in 79 AD?' (*The teacher now offers an immediate non-verbal signal, placing their forefinger over their lips to connotate 'no talking'. For one or two students who raise their hands, without talking, the teacher lifts their own hand and gestures a 'waves downwards' signal to suggest to students to put down their hands. This is done at the same time as their other hand and forefinger remaining placed over their lips to signal silence and thinking. All this data (happens) within ten seconds! The students have not spoken and have been given essential 'thinking time'. What now lies in front of the teacher is a mixture of students who are fully engaged in the process, with some who know the answer, others who are guessing and others who have no clue whatsoever. This happens every lesson in every classroom. Effective teachers always seek to reduce the latter and increase the former. Some are focused, and others not so. Whatever happens next, the teacher will now be able to determine what to do with the information.*)

Teacher: 'OK. Now, without talking, I'd like you to think about your answer once again. Even if you think it might be wrong, when I say "Go!", I want you to pair up and give me some evidence that you have *thought* about my question.' (*The students have still not spoken, disrupted the lesson or had a chance to say the answer.*)

Teacher: 'Before you tell me your answer, I'm going to give you one extra chance to think again, or change your mind. This time, you have ten seconds to pair up with your partner and say aloud (whisper) to one another your answer.' (*Long three-second pause.*) 'Go!'

Students: (*The classroom lights up with all students talking about the question. The teacher quickly scans the room to see that all students are participating and can now offer any microsecond interventions for any students off-task. The success here rests on the teacher ensuring this stage doesn't become too lengthy.*)

Teacher: (*After a delay of ten seconds, the teacher calls loudly:*) 'Five, four, three, two... one.' (*The teacher offers a routine countdown, and the students stop talking. The classroom becomes silent, and the teacher reminds the students of the process.*)

Teacher: 'Now, everyone. You have all had a moment to think about my question. I've asked you to think about it first, then you have had some time to share it with your partner. Next time, when I say "Write it down", I would like you to take your whiteboard and board pen and write down your answer. After these last ten seconds, I'll shout 'Show me'... and you will need to ensure that your whiteboard is facing me at the front with your final answer.'

(The teacher waits two seconds for students to settle and then, without hesitation, shouts 'Go!' – a non-verbal reminder to students that the teacher is in charge, despite the increase in excitement.)

Teacher: 'OK, go!'

Students: (The students take their board pen and begin to write their responses on the whiteboard. During this time, the teacher scans the room for interventions and interrupts the process ten seconds later with another countdown.)

Teacher: 'OK, show me!' (shouted. There is a high buzz in the room, and the teacher supports this stage with non-verbal signals: lifted eyebrows, waving upwards to suggest to some students to lift their whiteboards... They wait ten seconds and walk the room, not speaking.)

Many teachers will be able to picture this scene. The question is, do you fall into the trap explained in Scenario 1 or consciously use Scenario 2 as a teaching routine?

> **For more guidance on research-informed behaviour interventions to support the delivery of effective questioning, scan this QR code:**

Tweaking what you already do!

Using recommendations from cognitive science regarding retrieval practice (write it down, say it out aloud) is a more effective way to support learning that *all* teachers should use. Adding in the 'think it through' stage into Scenario 2 forces a period of silent reflection, and following this with 'write it down' before 'saying it out loud' is a more effective model for teaching. Insisting that all students then 'show me' at the end makes a simple teaching technique super-efficient. Doing so ensures that the teacher receives a much larger response and increases the success rate. By using 'show me!', it makes thinking more concrete. It makes the learning visible. The result? Rather than asking one student for a reply, the teacher made a couple of tweaks and created the conditions where all students were thinking and responding to their instruction. This is a much more efficient and effective method to use. Disclaimer: You may want students to reveal their answers one at a time rather than being overwhelmed by everyone's responses, which may increase your workload in the moment.

Scan this QR code to see a video breakdown explaining 'Think, Pair, Share, Show Me!'

TEMPLATE

This template outlines how best to use the mini whiteboards approach. Write down what you aim to do in your lesson, and when, on the right-hand side.

Mini whiteboards

Step	Description	Your Plan
1	Teacher frames expectations and sets up the activity.	
2	Teacher poses a question and signals for students to think silently.	
3	Teacher signals for students to share their answer with a partner.	
4	Teacher signals for students to write their answer on their mini whiteboard.	
5	Teacher signals for students to show their answer to the class.	
6	Teacher scans the room and provides feedback as needed.	

Scan this QR code to see a video of an alternate template for mini whiteboards.

Convergent questions

This provides a simple explanation of the different question types you can try using. Use this template to design your own questions and have them to hand in the classroom.

Question Type	Example Question	Explanation
Procedural	(Design and Technology lesson) How do you make a cup of tea? Write and draw each stage.	Questions that help guide students through the learning process and clarify instructions.
Convergent	(History lesson) Name the last three Prime Ministers of the United Kingdom.	Questions that typically have a single correct answer and assess students' knowledge and comprehension.
Divergent	(Art teacher) How might you use different colours and shapes to express different emotions in your artwork?	Open-ended questions that encourage students to think creatively and come up with multiple possible answers.
Evaluative	(English teacher) What are the strengths and weaknesses of X character in Y story?	Questions that help students to think critically and form opinions about historical events or issues.

CHAPTER 3
QUESTIONING TECHNIQUES FOR (OLDER) STUDENTS

Context, ability, age: Question delivery in secondary/further education

In this chapter, I discuss effective **questioning strategies for older students**, such as **cold calling**, used in secondary schools and further education establishments as students work towards their formal assessments. I will also discuss what types of questions are most effective in the classroom, including which questioning behaviours increase or interfere with student learning.

With questioning techniques in mind, it is worth flagging the research in 'Teacher questioning behavior and student learning: What research says to teachers' (Ellis, 1993). The author brings together research findings, their implications and guidelines for teachers who wish to make informed choices about improving their classroom questioning behaviour.

I would also like to highlight the use of alternative, non-questioning techniques. Wilen (1991) suggests that they 'may be more conducive than questioning techniques to stimulate student participation and thinking. Students responded to teacher statements as much as they do to their questions.' (p. 11). Non-questioning alternatives, including statements and wait time, resulted in more student participation and talking, peer-to-peer interaction and student questions.

EXPLAINER

Later in this chapter, we will unpick cold calling as a questioning technique. The technique of **cold calling** is a powerful tool – and, with a few adjustments, probably one of a teacher's greatest tools – in the context of students' learning in the teenage and early adult years. Most research suggests that questions motivate students and keep them on task, focusing their attention on what is to be learned. Teachers can use questions to elicit a depth of processing that is more effective than passive processing.

To be effective, teachers should use clear and concise questioning, relate questions to the subject matter and provide students with time to think before responding. Frequent factual recall questions, as well as questions that require higher cognitive processing, such as conceptual and evaluative questions, can be useful for specific teaching goals. However, there are also questioning behaviours that can interfere with student learning, including:

- interrupting students when they are speaking

- asking questions that are too difficult or unrelated to the subject matter

- making assumptions about students' knowledge or abilities

- ignoring students' questions or concerns

- giving too much or too little feedback

- failing to provide clear instructions or expectations

- not providing enough opportunities for students to practise or apply new skills

- not allowing students to take an active role in their learning

- and failing to address students' individual needs.

Furthermore, while non-academic questions and discussions are an important part of the social, emotional and mental health aspects of learning, they have **not** been found to increase student achievement. It is important to define student achievement beyond exam scores and consider the impact of education on other aspects of students' lives, such as their relationships with other adults and peers in a school setting. In summary, effective questioning techniques can motivate students' needs.

Doug Lemov's seminal text *Teach Like A Champion* (2010) offers 63 practical teaching techniques, with some helping teacher questioning to become more data-driven. I prefer the term 'assessment-driven' personally, because, essentially, a question should assess the learning and check for understanding. This allows the teacher to gather a wide range of data, defined in a number of ways, including written, verbal and non-verbal data in the classroom. But for now, let's return to the recommendations from 'Teacher questioning behavior and student learning' (Ellis, 1993).

Teacher-questioning behaviours

Probing student responses in a non-judgemental way, acknowledging correct responses from students and using praise specifically and discriminately are found to be powerful patterns for improving communication and student achievement.

Some of the research suggests that questions motivate students. They keep them on task and focus their attention on what is to be learned. The teacher's question is a 'cue to the student that the information required to answer the question is important' (Ellis, 1993, p. 3). Questions elicit a depth of processing rather than passive processing – for example, reading text alone. Questions activate metacognition, so that students become aware of how well they are mastering a topic or whether they need to study further, impacting learning gains. Developing a degree of mastery in the curriculum can be assessed by low-stakes quizzing and high-stakes assessment.

What types of questions are most effective in the classroom?

Using particular strategies can be effective for particular teaching goals. Systems have been developed by various researchers who have applied Bloom's taxonomy (1956) of thought processes at various cognitive levels (for example, Anderson and Krathwohl's (2001) create, evaluate, analyse, apply, understand and remember), with knowledge being a precursor for effectiveness. However, it's always worth keeping up-to-date with the available research, any claims, findings and how ideas have evolved. For example, Bloom's taxonomy fails to acknowledge other domains, including emotional, physical and cultural domains.

What questioning behaviours (types) are related to increases in student learning?

Factual recall questions: These use the lowest cognitive level but are most frequently used in classroom interactions. These questions are typically easy to identify and will ask students to name, identify, define, list or distinguish, for example. The emphasis is on memorisation and observation and the questions demonstrate that 90 per cent of student responses will be correct (Ellis, 1993). As with all research claims, do review the context.

Conceptual questions: These can be classified as convergent and divergent. Convergent questions, with only a single correct answer, take you to the next stage. Divergent questions, however, use open-ended thoughts to 'skilfully bring out new knowledge or unorthodox viewpoints about the topic under discussion' (Ellis, 1993, p. 5).

Evaluative questions: These are a mixture of all other levels of questions, to 'help students make value judgements about information or methods' (Ellis, 1993, p. 8).

What teacher-questioning behaviours influence student learning?

Phrase questions clearly: If ambiguous questions are posed, the probability of confusion is increased e.g. how long is a piece of string?

Relate questions to the subject matter: Although non-academic questions and discussions are an important part of the social, emotional and mental health (SEMH) aspects of learning, 'they have not been found to increase student achievement' (Ellis, 1993, p. 10). How do these research findings from 30 years ago compare to SEMH benefits today? It is frustrating that student achievement is typically defined by exam scores rather than, for example, a student improving their relationships with other adults and peers in a school setting. I do know that, from an autoethnographic point of view, when I put in a specific effort with an individual student and posed non-curriculum questions, there was some measurable impact on their participation in other aspects of their school life.

Use frequent factual recall questions: The emphasis is on memorisation and observation and these questions demonstrate that 90 per cent of student responses will be correct (Ellis, 1993).

Encourage student participation: Include responses from volunteers and non-volunteers, using discretion regarding the levels of difficulty. Increase student ownership; teachers tend to control discussions through their questioning, which hinders the freedom for students to participate, resulting in them feeling stifled (Wood and Wood, 1987, cited in Ellis, 1993).

What questions and behaviours interfere with student learning?

1. Interrupting students when they are speaking or trying to answer a question.

2. Asking a question that is too difficult or unrelated to the subject matter. This can be a precursor leading to escalated behaviours – for example, when a student opts out with a 'Don't know' response because they do not understand or wish to attempt to work out the solution.

3. Making assumptions about students' knowledge or abilities.

4. Ignoring students' questions or concerns.

5. Giving students too much or too little feedback.

6. Failing to provide clear instructions or expectations.

7. Not providing enough opportunities for students to practise or apply
new skills.

8. Not allowing students to take an active role in their learning.

9. Not addressing students' individual needs.

10. Failing to create and sustain a safe and supportive learning environment.

A case study of five high schools suggests that teacher questions limit discussion, whereas 'non-questioning alternatives foster discussion' (Dillon, 1985). In each case, 'students responded at greater length to the alternatives than to the questions'. When teachers provide explanations to student questions, it elicits further questions (i.e. thinking) and exploration from the students, compared to answering student questions (Dillon, 1985). In the context of older students discussed in this chapter, we know the classroom is a highly dynamic space, so it's worth considering a couple of these at points at any time for personal development.

PRACTICAL IDEA

Cold calling

Cold calling is a powerful questioning technique that can be used by teachers to encourage deeper thinking and accountability among all students in the classroom. In the **first of its kind** to academically critique the method, 'Cold calls to enhance class participation and student engagement' by Thulasidas and Gunawan (2022) investigates whether cold calling improves student engagement in classrooms. The study was conducted over seven weeks with 114 students, using a random script to select students for cold calls during class. The research suggested that, on average, cold calling **improves** class participation and student engagement when implemented with a structured approach and the right intentions.

When using the technique, there are several practical tips that teachers can follow. By following these tips, teachers can use cold calling effectively and help all students to think more deeply and engage more fully in their learning.

1. **Use datasets:** Use the technique to pose one question to a larger audience, allowing the teacher to gather a larger dataset of information. This increases your sample size and progression on the topics being taught.

2. **Use statistical sampling:** Question a sample of students to gather information from across the spectrum, using data from mixed-ability students.

3. **Ensure reliability:** Respond to correct answers with follow-up 'why' and 'how' questions – known as 'stretch it' questions – to ensure that you gather the best data on whether a student is likely to get a similar problem right the next time around. This avoids any false positives (lucky guesses!).

4. **Improve validity:** Make sure that the question asked receives a positive result as an effective measure of what students are trying to master. Align questions to check for understanding, matching the questions to the level of difficulty that would appear on an examination paper. Teachers should measure what they say they are measuring!

5. **Encourage all students to participate:** Ensure that everyone pays attention and develop a system in which all students think it is possible that they are about to be called, regardless of whether they have raised their hand. This will encourage all students to prepare to answer and think more deeply.

6. **Hold every student accountable:** Use cold calling alongside 'no opt out' or 'pose, pause, pounce, bounce' (both in Chapter 1) to encourage all students to think more deeply and hold every child in the classroom accountable in a lesson.

7. **Use appropriate techniques for the age group:** Be mindful that cold calling may not be an effective technique in some educational sectors, such as an Early Years classroom.

8. **Manage who gets to participate and think:** Do not default to the 'one question, one person responds' approach, which ensures that one child in the entire class is thinking, but not everyone else. We want everybody to pay attention and be thinking of responses in case they are called on to answer.

Based on some of the research findings that I have shared, I would recommend:

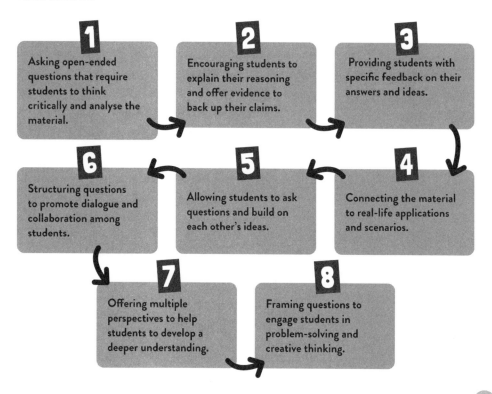

1 Asking open-ended questions that require students to think critically and analyse the material.

2 Encouraging students to explain their reasoning and offer evidence to back up their claims.

3 Providing students with specific feedback on their answers and ideas.

6 Structuring questions to promote dialogue and collaboration among students.

5 Allowing students to ask questions and build on each other's ideas.

4 Connecting the material to real-life applications and scenarios.

7 Offering multiple perspectives to help students to develop a deeper understanding.

8 Framing questions to engage students in problem-solving and creative thinking.

1. Questions should be open-ended to encourage reflection.

2. Ensure that all students think it's possible that they might be called on to answer.

3. Give careful consideration to whom you choose to answer the questions and when.

4. Cold calling a mixed-ability sample of students provides great feedback regarding the understanding of the class as a whole.

WORKED EXAMPLE

The cold call technique is a powerful way in which to engage all students in a secondary classroom or further education setting. It involves the teacher asking questions and calling on students to answer, regardless of whether they have raised their hands. Here are some practical ideas for implementing this technique effectively:

1. Pose open-ended questions that require critical thinking and analysis. For example, 'What are some of the causes and effects of climate change?'

2. Encourage students to explain their reasoning and provide evidence to support their answers. For example, 'Can you explain why you think that?' However, this elaboration question does move you (deeper) away from the factual cold call method.

3. Provide specific feedback on students' answers and ideas. For example, 'I like how you connected the causes and effects of climate change. Can you elaborate on that point?'

4. Connect the material to real-life applications and scenarios. For example, 'How does climate change affect our daily lives?'

5. Allow students to ask questions and build on each other's ideas. For example, 'Does anyone have a different perspective on this?'

6. Structure questions to promote dialogue and collaboration among students. For example, 'What are some ways we can work together to reduce our carbon footprint?'

7. Offer multiple perspectives to help students to develop a deeper understanding. For example, 'What are some arguments for and against renewable energy sources?'

8. Frame questions to engage students in problem-solving and creative thinking. For example, 'How can we design a more sustainable city?'

By implementing these ideas, teachers can use the cold call technique to create an engaging and interactive classroom environment where all students are encouraged to participate and think critically.

TEMPLATE

Cold calling

Scan the QR code to watch a video example of how to use the cold calling technique.

Here's a step-by-step procedure which you can put into your plan until you reach a point where you can automate the cold call technique effectively and to the point of automaticity.

Steps	Tips for Effective Cold Call Technique
Step 1	Use pre-planned ideas to pose one question to a large audience, allowing the teacher to gather a larger dataset of information.
Step 2	Use statistical sampling to question select students to gather information from across the spectrum, using data from mixed-ability students.
Step 3	Ensure reliability by responding to correct answers with follow-up 'why' and 'how' questions – something called 'stretch it' questions – to ensure that you gather the best data on whether a student is likely to get a similar problem right the next time around.
Step 4	Improve validity by making sure that the question asked receives a positive result as an effective measure of what students are trying to master. Use questions to check for understanding, aligning the questions to the level of difficulty that would appear on an examination paper or end of scheme assessments.
Step 5	Encourage all students to participate by developing a system that ensures all students think it is possible that they are about to be called, regardless of whether they have raised their hand. This will encourage all students to prepare to answer and think more deeply.

Step 6	Hold every student accountable by using cold call alongside 'no opt out' or 'pose, pause, pounce, bounce' to encourage all students to think more deeply.
Step 7	Use appropriate techniques for the age group by being mindful that cold call may not be an effective technique in some educational sectors such as an Early Years classroom.
Step 8	Manage who gets to participate and think by not defaulting to the 'one question, one person responds' approach, which ensures one child in the entire class is thinking, but not everyone else. You want everybody to pay attention and develop a system that ensures all students think it is possible that they are about to be called, regardless of whether they have raised their hand.

CHAPTER 4
QUESTIONING INFLUENCES

Environment: Socratic questioning – influences + success

This chapter looks at the **influence of external and internal factors** on the effectiveness of questioning approaches, delivery and response in a school classroom. How do external and internal influences determine how effective a question is received and answered in a school classroom? How does the environment in the classroom make a difference? How does the teacher's expertise determine the quality of the question?

All these questions are significant if we wish to get a deeper understanding of what a teacher needs to know, acquire and deploy in various contexts.

The chapter also looks at **Socratic questioning** , which is defined in the Explainer section. In the practical idea section, we also outline questioning ability in the context of **behaviour, scripting, setting the scene and metacognition**.

'Can feedback improve teaching?' (Coe, 1998) gives an insight into how feedback can improve performance and we will look into these insights throughout this chapter. In another study on the demotivational effect on retrospective rewards (Robinson, Gallus, Lee and Rogers, 2018) the researchers suggest that the retrospective awards may have sent unintended signals to the students, telling them that they were performing better than the descriptive social norm of their peers, and exceeding the institutional expectations for the awarded behaviour. In other words, the feedback received (reward) had a negative impact on student attendance!

It is important for teachers to understand the various conditions that impact feedback, such as the task and performance being measured, the type of feedback, the individual characteristics of the person receiving it, and the timing of feedback. Feedback is not consigned to written marking. It also includes how a teacher feeds back about any piece of work, including responding in the lesson to commentary.

Ultimately, there is a range of external and internal influences that determine how effectively a question is received and answered in a school classroom, and these influences are listed in the graphic below.

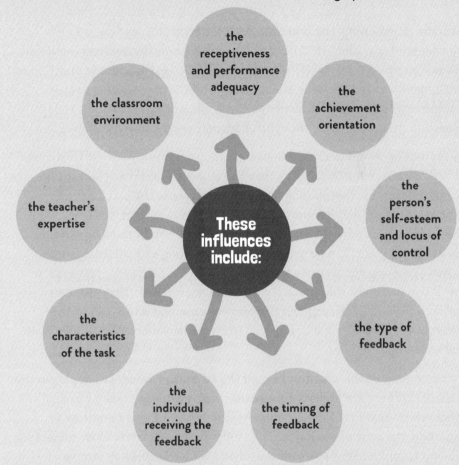

You should be aware of these different feedback influences when providing feedback to students. Furthermore, research has shown that written feedback is not the most reliable way to evaluate the learning process, as verbal feedback can be captured in the moment (though it is more difficult to evaluate). Therefore, it is important to consider the classroom influences at large which we will do throughout the chapter.

EXPLAINER

Socratic questioning, the practical idea offered in this section, is a very popular strategy. Once described as 'the most powerful teaching tactic for fostering critical thinking' (Paul and Elder, 2006, p. 2), Socratic questioning has long influenced teaching and learning, and the process of repeated questioning to elicit tacit knowledge is still influencing classrooms today. Question design provokes thoughtful answers and further questions.

In 'promoting students' critical thinking through Socratic method' (Dalim et al., 2022), the research suggests that 'the student's readiness [to respond to questions] is a... contributing factor that influences the participation of students' (p. 1041). Teachers reported high positivity that 'such [a] method has great potential in enhancing students' critical thinking skills' (p. 1044). Students can be actively involved in giving and discussing ideas, as well as making connections and expanding on their answers – essentially metacognitive skills. The research acknowledges, however, that 'teachers still face challenges carrying out the Socrative method effectively in their classrooms' (p. 1044), due to a lack of student motivation and teachers' skills and knowledge.

In the context of this chapter, I would like to discuss influences at play in the classroom. There are endless contextual factors when we seek to evaluate 'what works' best in our classrooms. As ever, what is being taught, your expertise, the time of year, what the students already know, what subject is being taught and the age of the students are all just a small sample of variations. For specificity, I would like to discuss influences from a **'feedback' perspective during questioning in class**.

In 'Can feedback improve teaching?', Coe (1998) looks at how feedback can improve performance. The purpose was to determine whether people who receive feedback on a task perform better than those who do not, and whether any empirical evidence supports it. Coe (1998) notes the conditions that impact feedback as:

1. the type of task and which performance is being measured

2. the characteristics of the particular feedback that is given, and the way in which it is given

3. the individual characteristics of the person receiving the feedback.

Coe (1998) highlights 16 specific feedback variables:

1. the characteristic of the task and any distinction between motivation and effort and its links to performance

2. how feedback is presented, especially goal-setting

3. ego involvement (e.g. competition)

4. self-evaluation

5. norm-referenced or self-referenced

6. informational or controlling

7. positive or negative feedback

8. timing (immediate or delayed)

9. general or focused

10. credibility (containing accurate information)

11. level of involvement

12. self-efficacy and self-esteem – studies reveal that students with high self-esteem improved with positive feedback compared to those with low self-esteem (Ilgen et al., 1979)

13. attributions for success and failure

14. locus of control (Rotter, 1966) – the differences between individuals and their expectations about the relationship between their own behaviour and the reinforcement that they receive

15. achievement orientation

16. receptiveness and performance adequacy.

What do these influences mean for teachers?

These influences can help teachers to understand the best way in which to provide feedback to their students, taking into account the individual characteristics of the student, the type of task and the characteristics of the feedback. For example, teachers can use positive feedback to increase self-esteem in students with lower self-esteem or provide immediate feedback for tasks that require quick responses. Additionally, teachers can set goals for students and provide information that is accurate and tailored to the individual student, to increase the effectiveness of their feedback.

We can also use these influences to better understand how to conduct intelligent accountability as part of our quality assurance processes in our schools. This not only ensures that our children's needs are met, but it also helps to reduce sweeping generalisations about the performances of others.

PRACTICAL IDEA

Scripts and Socratic questioning

We will now discuss questioning ability from the perspective of behaviour, scripting, setting the scene and metacognition. I've offered a brief explanation of each:

1. **Behaviour:** Questioning is one of the quickest ways of holding a student to account, whether for developing knowledge or for helping students to remain focused when managing behaviour. We know that the teacher must establish clear routines and an effective climate for learning. Only then can they use some powerful tools to deliver highly effective questions.

2. **Scripting:** To help teachers to reduce workload and develop a methodology that can be part of the teacher's DNA, it's essential that teachers learn how to use scripts, which are very similar to mnemonics. This will help them to recall detailed information using a simple acronym, thereby establishing an effective routine and reducing workload. Without listing the numerous acronyms across the teaching profession, one simple strategy with which many will be familiar is the acronym PPPB – pose, pause, pounce, bounce – as explained in Chapter 1.

3. **Setting the scene:** Using the encode-store-retrieve methodology (see Chapter 2), inspired by cognitive science, teachers can help to set the scene, supporting students to decode and process information at the consolidation stage of learning. This happens between the 'encode' and 'store' stages of learning. Teachers can tell stories that help to bring difficult curriculum content to life, or they can develop scripts to help explain both familiar and new information in the context of the classroom.

4. **Metacognition:** This is the ability to think about and control one's own thinking, and it plays a critical role in learning, problem-solving and decision-making.

Executive function refers to a set of mental processes that are responsible for controlling and coordinating other cognitive abilities and behaviours, allowing us to set goals, plan and execute actions, monitor progress, and adjust our behaviour in response to changing circumstances. Some of the key components of executive function include:

1. **working memory:** the ability to hold and manipulate information in your mind over short periods of time

2. **cognitive flexibility:** the ability to switch between different tasks or mental sets, and to adjust your behaviour in response to changing demands

3. **inhibition:** the ability to suppress impulses or automatic responses that may interfere with achieving a goal

4. **planning and organisation:** the ability to create and follow a plan of action to achieve a goal, including breaking down complex tasks into smaller steps

5. **time management:** the ability to prioritise tasks, manage time effectively and meet deadlines.

Executive function is important for many aspects of daily life, including academic and occupational success, interpersonal relationships and emotional regulation. It develops gradually throughout childhood and continues to improve into young adulthood, but can be affected by various factors such as stress, sleep deprivation and neurological disorders.

Socratic questioning

Socratic questioning is a popular and well-documented technique, discussed in this book to ensure that using this method becomes one of the most-used tools in a teacher's classroom toolkit. Socratic questioning helps to promote independent and critical thinking for students. The teacher offers probing questions that require students to use higher-order thinking skills, such as evaluation, analysis and synthesis of information.

SOCRATIC QUESTIONING INVOLVES THE TEACHER ADOPTING FOUR ROLES:

1. **Gadfly:** This is a fly that jumps on livestock to feed on their blood, faeces or bacteria. The term was used by Plato (428BC) to describe Socrates (469BC) acting uncomfortably during the Athenian political scene. Socrates was known as a gadfly because his questions were often seen as challenging or controversial, and he often criticised the existing social order. He was a nuisance to the powerful and wealthy and was seen as a threat to their established authority. He often challenged the status quo and encouraged people to think critically and independently, which was seen as a threat to the existing power structure. At this stage during the Socratic questioning process, the teacher asks multiple probing questions to dig deeper to learn what the student knows or does not know.

2. **Midwife:** This is the supportive and encouraging phase in order to 'give birth' or to 'deliver' new ideas for the student and others to consider.

3. **Stingray:** This large fish, related to sharks, has venom in its tail. In the classroom, a teacher asks a direct question to introduce a 'venomous shock' to the discussion, moving the conversation in a new direction or perspective.

4. **Uninformed:** The teacher at this stage pretends that they know absolutely nothing about the topic, to encourage students to elaborate on what they know or self-explain new information. Elaboration and self-explanation are two very important study skills:

   - *elaboration:* generating an explanation for why

   - *self-explanation:* explaining how new information is related to known information, or explaining steps taken during problem-solving.

I'd like to offer an adaptation of this technique in a mnemonic form that will help you to remember the four roles. I have used the letters M, A, L and I (abbreviated to match the West African country Mali to help you to remember) for the four roles above. This acronym will help not only to reduce workload but also to automate the process, alongside an established bank of questions and techniques.

1. **M for Mosquito:** Similar to a mosquito, the teacher here asks lots of short and pointed questions. These can be a mixture of closed questions to elicit a 'Yes' or 'No' response, or a simple retort: 'Explain to me why you think this...'

2. **A for Affectionate:** Like a parent or family member, this stage acts like a close relative to help to support and encourage the formation of new ideas.

3. **L for Laceration:** Following on from the above stages, the teacher would then offer a shock to the process – similar to a 'curve ball', where new, unexpected and relevant (to the learning process) information is offered. For example, 'Did you know that there are X number of questions posed in this book, including this one?' (See page 157 for the actual number of questions posed!)

4. **I for Ignorant:** Finally, to leave students with further inquiry and opportunities for new learning (homework), if the teacher poses the 'laceration' stage to offer a shock, following a discussion with students the teacher could pose a large number of concluding questions and plead ignorance at this stage, encouraging students to go off and find out answers during a classroom task and/or homework activity.

1. A script, like a mnemonic, provides a simple acronym to help establish and remember an effective questioning routine.

2. Socratic questioning uses probing questions to develop students' critical thinking skills.

3. Use the MALI technique to reduce your workload and automate your questioning process.

WORKED EXAMPLE

Here are a set of gadfly, midwife, stingray and uninformed example questions, based on the 'Reported road casualties Great Britain: e-Scooter factsheet 2021' (Department for Transport, 2021) which could be used as a discussion in the classroom:

Gadfly 1 = Should scooters be made illegal on pavements?

Gadfly 2 = Should scooters be made illegal in local parks?

Midwife 1 = What if the speed on scooters was limited?

Midwife 2 = What if all scooters had automatic lights and warning bells?

Stingray 1 = Did you know that 10 people have been killed on e-Scooters?

Stingray 2 = Did you know men are more likely to be in an e-Scooter accident than women?

Uniformed 1 = What's the point of a scooter?

Uniformed 2 = Does a scooter need petrol?

Earlier in this chapter, we learned how questioning can be improved using scripts or mnemonics, setting the scene through the encode-store-retrieve methodology, and promoting metacognition by encouraging students to think about their own thinking processes, using the Socratic questioning technique and the four roles described above, adapted as the mnemonic MALI.

M for Mosquito
A for Affectionate
L for Laceration
I for Ignorant

Here is a role play demonstrating how the MALI technique can be used in a Key Stage 3 geography lesson on types of rivers:

Mosquito

This is the 'pointed question' stage.

Teacher: 'Can anyone tell me what a river is?'

Student 1: 'A river is a natural flowing watercourse.'

Teacher: 'Good. And what's the difference between a river and a stream?'

Student 2: 'A stream is a smaller body of water that flows into a river.'

Teacher: 'Excellent. Can you name a famous river in the world?'

Student 3: 'The Amazon River.'

Teacher: 'Very good. Now, can you tell me one interesting fact about the Amazon River?'

Affectionate

Like a parent or family member, this stage acts like a close relative to help to support and encourage.

Teacher: 'Great job, everyone. You're all doing really well with your understanding of rivers. Keep up the good work and remember, I'm here to support you in any way I can. Which is longer: the River Nile or the Amazon River?'

Laceration

This stage is where the teacher would then offer a shock to the process, similar to a 'curve ball', where new, unexpected and relevant (to the learning process) information is offered.

Teacher: 'Did you know that there are over 165 major rivers in the world? That's a lot of rivers to learn about! So, let's focus on the five major types of rivers and what makes them unique.'

Ignorant

This stage leaves students with further inquiry and opportunities for new learning.

Teacher: 'OK, class, we've covered a lot of ground today. But before we wrap up, I want to leave you with some questions to consider for homework. What are the primary types of rivers and what makes them different from each other? What are some of the most important rivers in the world and how do they impact the communities around them? I look forward to hearing your thoughts on these questions in our next lesson.'

TEMPLATE

Gadfly, midwife, stingray, uninformed

This template helps you plan how to approach Socratic questioning to promote independent and critical thinking. Write down the questions you might ask for a particular topic.

Stage	Role	Example Question
1	Gadfly *The probing stage*	
2	Midwife *The supportive stage*	
3	Stingray *The shock tactic stage*	
4	Uninformed *The elaborative stage*	

MALI

This template helps you plan how to approach Socratic questioning to promote independent and critical thinking. Write down the questions you might ask for a particular topic.

Step	Role	Example Question
1	M = Mosquito *The pointed question stage*	
2	A = Affectionate *The encouraging stage*	
3	L = Laceration *The curveball stage*	
4	I = Ignorant *The inquiry stage*	

CHAPTER 5
QUESTIONING AND (META) COGNITION

Cognition and working memory

This chapter will explore how questioning can be used in the classroom and how it is related to thinking and understanding, which we call **cognition and metacognition**. One way in which questioning can encourage metacognition is to use **funnel questions**. My interest in how the brain works, and why I believe that all teachers should know about it too, will highlight why asking and formatting good questions is really important for teachers; this chapter will explore how to do this well.

Teachers must help students to move from being a beginner to becoming an expert, and part of this is learning how to manage their own learning. Students need to know how to choose the best way in which to solve a problem, and this is called 'self-regulation'. This chapter will evaluate different ways of asking questions in the classroom to help students to remember what they learn and know how to use that learning in new situations. The overall goal is to help teachers to support their students to think about their own thinking and make good choices about how learning happens.

EXPLAINER

In 'Questioning the questions' research by Tienken et al. (2009), academics reference 'historical accounts of questioning used in the education process' (p. 39), traced back to Socrates – that is, how questions can be posed to help reflect and think critically about the subject in order to come to a new understanding. Over the course of my teaching career, I have received some nuggets of wisdom on questioning, but nothing formally in my teacher training, **nor anything exclusively dedicated to questioning** until the last decade of my classroom career. How do we therefore raise the profile of effective questioning? The challenge is to understand the type of training that would be most useful to target.

In the article 'Self-questioning – an aid to metacognition', Williamson (1996, p. 45) suggests that 'when students are directly taught appropriate self-questioning techniques through modelling, followed by scaffolding instruction, and metacognitive strategy employment, [their] interaction is enhanced'. Therefore, the focus on continuous attention to self-generated questions places the 'locus of control' (Rotter, 1966) on students.

Recently I discovered the research on 'locus of control' in reference to some work that I was researching on feedback. As teachers, it is preferable to move away from our fixation on marking and feedback towards written, verbal and non-verbal feedback, feed-forward and feed-up. The 'locus of control' was designed to assess the difference between individuals and their expectations – expectations about the relationship between their own behaviour and the reinforcement that they receive – meaning that students control the consequences of their behaviour and/or learning.

In research published more recently, 'Using collaborative action research to enhance differentiated instruction' (Dulfer et al., 2021) sought to understand how teachers enacted differentiation (also known as adaptive teaching or scaffolding) in the classroom. In the research, teachers opted to focus on improving metacognition and questioning techniques. One of the techniques used was 'cubing', as described in 'How to differentiate instruction in mixed ability classrooms' (Tomlinson, 2001, p. 81):

'To help his students think about and make sense of these ideas, [the teacher] uses cubing. Each six-sided cube carries these instructions for students: describe, compare, tell your feelings about, tell the parts of, use, and tell the good and bad things about.'

The teacher assigns each student either a blue cube (working at or below level) or a green cube (performing above or well above level), depending on their current level of understanding. The research concludes that some teachers, having consulted research-informed publications on questioning, reflected 'more deeply on their approach to dialogic teaching' (Dulfer et al., 2021, p. 12). The research revealed how professional development can empower teachers 'to reflect on practice and enact new strategies' (p. 12) to address student needs and can improve teachers' ability to improve their differentiated instruction techniques, including questioning. Developing metacognition, asking students to question why and how they are doing things, with questions like 'Why is that useful to [your assessment task]?' is something that can become automatic for teachers. Dulfer et al. (2021, p. 8) also identified that 'observations and discussions drew attention to habitual teaching strategies, which were invisible to the teacher until someone else noted them'.

PRACTICAL IDEA

Funnel questions

In a relatively new book, *The Teaching and Learning Playbook: Examples of Excellence in Teaching*, Feely and Karlin (2022) provide a comprehensive overview of 100 techniques that teachers can use to bring about improvements in their schools. Cleverly designed to support routines, questioning, modelling and curriculum development, the book is a reminder to all that the quality of teaching is the greatest factor affecting student achievement. Inside the questioning and checking for understanding section, over 20 techniques are offered with one pertinent point. Any teacher can compose a wide number and variety of questions, but they must learn some strategies to check for understanding, not from just one student, but from all the students in front of them (see Chapter 2, think, pair, share).

One key questioning strategy to help to develop student metacognition is asking funnel questions.

Funnel questions are a series of increasingly specific questions that start with broad questions and gradually become more focused. The process obtains higher levels of detail as the conversation moves through a sequence to become more refined: moving from open questions to probing questions and then moving to very closed questions.

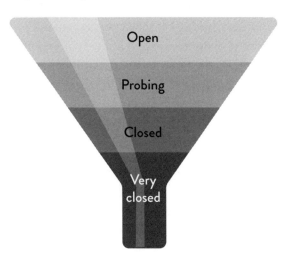

Examples of funnel questions include:

1. What is your current challenge? (Open question)

2. What have you tried so far to address this challenge? (Probing)

3. What is your timeline for finding a solution? (Closed)

4. What is your budget for this project? (Very closed)

5. How do you make decisions on projects like this? (Open/probing)

Teacher-designed questions that ask students to think about their learning process are essential metacognitive strategies for teachers to deploy. There is much value in teaching through questioning, especially to elicit critical thinking in young people. Key study skills that must be taught include **self-explanation** and **elaboration** as part of the learning process.

What is self-explanation as a study skill?

Self-explanation is a study skill that involves actively explaining material to yourself as you read or watch a lecture. It involves summarising the material, highlighting key points and forming connections between different pieces of information.

What is elaboration as a study skill?

Elaboration is a study skill that involves taking information from a lecture or something you have read and adding more details to it. It involves making connections between different topics and using examples to explain difficult concepts. Elaboration is a study skill that involves expanding and building upon new information in order to deepen understanding and improve retention. It is a cognitive process that helps learners connect new material with existing knowledge, making it easier to remember and apply.

How can these techniques help to promote metacognition for students?

These techniques can help to promote metacognition for students by allowing them to think critically about their learning. Self-explanation and elaboration help students to reflect on their learning, understand the material more deeply and make connections between different topics. This can help them to develop a better understanding of the material and be able to recall it more effectively. However, they must be taught these skills.

Using effective questioning, such as funnel questions, allows a teacher to retrieve information from students, thereby supporting retention and storage. By drawing out detailed responses from students, material can be reviewed to ensure that students have retained it. This allows teachers to assess student understanding and provide targeted feedback. Let's unpick a range of questions and strategies to deploy using this technique.

Stage 1

The teacher asks lots of open-ended questions and actively listens to the responses. These types of questions are more likely to generate complete answers, but may elicit less accurate information on more specific questions. Using an open-ended question is always a good way to kick-start a conversation; it is designed to gather more complete information to identify meaningful ideas to be explored later. Depending on how the student responds, the teacher can 'obtain not only information about *what* is said and *how* it is said, but also what is *not* said' (Matsumoto et al., 2015, p. 9). Experienced professionals will be able to evaluate a student's verbal and non-verbal behaviours when they respond to more direct closed questions.

Stage 2

As the student replies, during active observation the teacher can pose what, who, when, where, why and how type questions in response to a student's answer. These types of questions allow the teacher to assess the initial response, considering how to ask follow-up questions. For example, 'Tell me more about...'

Stage 3

As topics are prioritised in the conversation, 'engaging in a delicate balance of asking both open and closed-ended questions' (Matsumoto et al., 2015, p. 9), inquiry becomes more narrow and closed as the teacher elicits more detailed information – rather like peeling away one layer of an onion skin towards the centre. It is important to uncover information by gradually narrowing the focus. The more specific the question, the more information is gleaned, which in turn leads towards more specific responses.

Stage 4

The final stage is layering: the careful choice of words during the information-gathering phase. When teachers pose questions, they can rapidly become embroiled in bias and emotion-laden words. These recommendations highlight how effective conversations can occur (or not) in order to develop and maintain rapport with a particular person.

Layering might look like this:

This example maximises the value of open and closed-ended questions.

1. To use the funnel technique, start with open-ended questions and move through probing questions towards closed-ended questions.

2. Open-ended questions allow you to gain detailed information to be explored later, as well as information about what is not said.

3. Think of the technique as like peeling an onion, narrowing the focus as you get closer to the centre to elicit more specific responses.

WORKED EXAMPLE

Example 1

This example uses the funnel question technique in an English lesson in a secondary school. The students have been studying Macbeth and they are analysing some of the characters in the play. How would the teacher use the funnel question technique?

Teacher: 'Let's start by discussing the character of Macbeth. What do you think his key character traits are?' (*Open question*)

Student 1: 'I think he's ambitious and power-hungry.'

Teacher: 'That's interesting. Can you tell me more about his ambition?' (*Probing question*)

Student 2: 'Well, he's willing to do whatever it takes to get what he wants, even if it means killing people.'

Teacher: 'Great. Can you give me an example of when he shows this ambition?' (*Closed question*)

Student 3: 'Yeah, he kills Duncan in order to become king.'

Teacher: 'What do you think motivates him to take such drastic measures?' (*Open question*)

Student 4: 'I think he's driven by his own ego and pride. He wants to prove himself and be seen as successful.'

Teacher: 'That's an interesting point. Why do you think his ego is so important to him?' (*Probing question*)

Student 5: 'I think he's trying to prove that he's better than everyone else and that he can achieve anything he sets his mind to.'

Example 2

This is a role-play script between a classroom teacher and a group of students.

Teacher: 'Let's start off by discussing the current project you're working on. What is the challenge you're facing?' (*Open question*)

Students: 'We're having trouble figuring out the best way to present our findings.'

Teacher: 'OK, what have you tried so far to address this challenge?' (*Probing question*)

Students: 'We've been brainstorming different ideas, but we're not sure which one is the best.'

Teacher: 'That's great. What is your timeline for finding a solution?' (*Closed question*)

Students: 'We'd like to have it done by the end of the month.'

Teacher: 'What is your budget for this project?' (*Very closed question*)

Students: 'We're not sure yet, but we have some ideas for how to fund it.'

Teacher: 'How do you make decisions on projects like this?' (*Open/probing question*)

Students: 'We like to discuss our ideas and come to a consensus before making a decision.'

TEMPLATE

Funnel questions: Teacher classroom problem/discussion

Use this template to plan open/closed questions and potential ways of responding. For specific topics, add a definition to support your teaching, including how you might rephrase your conversations.

Question	Response
1. Open question	
2. Rephrase with specific component	
3. Add definition	
4. Rephrase with specificity and definition	
5. Pose closed question	

CHAPTER 6
QUESTIONING IN AN ONLINE CONTEXT

Online teaching

This chapter focuses on **questioning techniques for online teaching**. Learning the lessons from the COVID-19 pandemic, it is important to ensure that all teachers are trained in delivering online learning and that students can access and understand the technology. The Education Endowment Foundation (EEF, 2020) published a rapid evidence assessment guide on remote learning, which identified five key research findings:

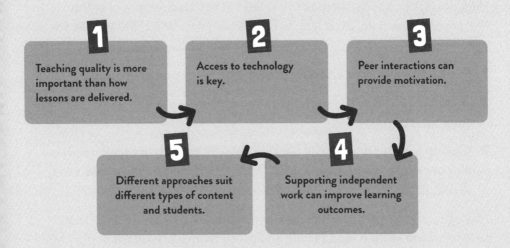

1 Teaching quality is more important than how lessons are delivered.

2 Access to technology is key.

3 Peer interactions can provide motivation.

5 Different approaches suit different types of content and students.

4 Supporting independent work can improve learning outcomes.

A study by Choi et al. (2005) revealed that scaffolding questioning strategies could facilitate reflective thinking in online small group discussions. This chapter will explore the key questioning technique of **ABC – agree, build, challenge** – and provide worked examples and templates to help teachers to use this technique effectively in their online teaching.

EXPLAINER

A strategy that can help teachers to work more effectively online is using 'lecture pauses'. 'A lecture pause occurs when instructor-talk stops, and students are asked to think about their learning and what they will do with it' (Rice, 2018). The evidence argues that 'these lecture pauses not only benefit the students by allowing them a chance to relate and recall, but it also benefits the instructors' (Arnold, 2020, p.4).

In a journal article from 2020, Michelle Arnold writes that 'Pauses can be used in the traditional classroom to help students focus, understand what they have been taught, apply it to their own lives, and have an overall more enjoyable learning experience.' (p. 6) She also states that 'When students are given the opportunity to direct their own learning on a topic, make connections, and evaluate ideas in a safe and welcoming environment with their peers, their opportunities to succeed in the classroom and in the life increase.' (Arnold, 2020, p. 5) Three categories of lecture pauses are presented:

1. Starting pauses 'grab attention, focus, and break preoccupation'.

2. A midpause 'allows the students to remember, apply, and understand what they have learned'.

3. Closing pauses are powerful because they 'help students accomplish but also because of when they occur'. (Rice, 2018, quoted in Arnold, 2020, p. 5)

Having read this research, the questions that I ask myself are: If all that teachers need to do is stop talking and pause to improve retention for their students, why don't they do this more often? How should we do this in the physical and virtual classroom in a meaningful way?

At the pandemic's peak, the University of Manitoba published 12 tips for pivoting to teaching in a virtual environment (Collins et al., 2020):

Tip 1: Review learning objectives

Think critically about what can realistically be achieved. How could you start the lesson off with an opening question?

Tip 2: Review resources

Effective integration of digital tools and technologies is facilitated by teachers who explore and learn technologies. What online software could you use that quizzes your students to retrieve past information?

Tip 3: Explore strategies to engage learners

Forging positive connections with teachers has been shown to play a significant role in student satisfaction. What questions could you use to facilitate discussion?

Tip 4: Design educational content for use online

Teachers can remove extraneous cognitive load that distracts from the learning process. They can enhance cognitive load by planning activities that focus on retrieval practice – that is, retrieving the learned information to apply it and also removing irrelevant information. Strategies could include:

1. Allowing students to 'self-explain' the material being presented.

2. When using active learning activities, ensure adequate variability.

What elaboration or self-explanation questions could you pose to reinforce learning?

Tip 5: Consider using diverse teaching strategies

Using a variety of learning technologies will not only help teachers to appeal to different students, but it also teaches students how to use a range of technology and helps them to maximise their engagement. What different questioning strategies could work in an online environment?

Tip 6: Maximise what the technology can do

Breakout rooms during an online lecture can facilitate the development and maintenance of learner relationships. How could you start this process with a key question to guide the group's focus?

Tip 7: Determine the purpose of assessment

The use of authentic and other formative assessments in online contexts facilitates greater interaction and engagement with the delivery of the feedback, through online discussions, peer reviews using shared documents, written feedback, synchronous or asynchronous video. How could you integrate multiple-choice questions to support retention? Remember, research on multiple choice questions suggests that the choices offered should be very similar to increase retrieval strength and help eliminate wrong answers. For example, what is tomato ketchup – a sauce, a star or a tree?

Tip 8: Refine assessments to reflect virtual environments

Refinements for virtual environments may include combining or splitting assessments to ensure that they cover the necessary level of mastery for each learning objective, as well as providing an opportunity for the learner to scaffold throughout the course. What quizzing software could you use for an online environment? There are so many to choose from. Make sure their marketing claims are backed by education research!

Tip 9: Familiarisation with virtual teaching

It is recommended that materials are distributed to students ahead of time, with encouragement for them to play with the technology beforehand. In the field of cognitive science, this is known as priming. How could you design pre- and post-lesson scenarios where students could watch a question posed by the teacher? For example, they could scan a QR code or click on a link before or after a lesson. The effect of short instructional videos impacts greatly on students' learning (Ding et al., 2022).

Tip 10: Keep the environment safe and respectful

Have an open and frank discussion of etiquette to establish standards and protocols for interacting within the virtual environment. What reoccurring questions could you pose to reinforce learning expectations?

Tip 11: Have a back-up plan

Develop strategies and plans to be ready for when there are issues with technology. What happens if everything stops working? How do you keep the learning moving? I always start off by signposting plan B before commencing any online session.

Tip 12: Maintain some compassion for transition to remote learning

Social supports within remote learning contexts can be facilitated through regular group study assignments that encourage small group actions and cooperation, and may lead to socialisation outside of the course. What key assessment question could you pose to offer encouragement?

All teachers must reflect on curriculum delivery in virtual environments, deploying teaching strategies grounded in learning theory germane to virtual teaching environments, such as cognitive load theory.

Here is some other useful research conducted during the pandemic. Scan the QR codes to learn more about each of the below studies:

A teacher's gaze in video lectures improves learning

Does size matter?

How can teachers teach better online?

Creating a supportive, online environment for students

Safeguarding students: Teaching students using Zoom video

Can teachers use what they know about cognitive science and successfully apply it to remote teaching?

Although I was not working in a school at the peak of the pandemic, I was working with teachers all across the world. At the beginning of the pandemic, I was 'teaching' teachers in Vietnam at 5.00 am and then working with teachers in Brazil at 4.00 pm – the equivalent of last thing in the day in Ho Chi Minh City and first thing in the morning in Rio de Janeiro. With this 'time of day' context, the number of people participating and the technology available to me at the time, my priorities were how I presented new information or consolidated things that we had already covered, to help me to understand what the teachers participating knew (or didn't know). The technology allowed me as a teacher-presenter to quiz the audience through surveys, animations and quizzing software. Factoring in how I presented the material and the technology I chose to use, I wonder how much time I spent thinking deeply about the questions that I posed to the audience. Whether asking questions in an online environment or in the classroom, key questions must be considered to facilitate thinking and reflection or, just as important, to enable the teacher to determine what 'students' know by quizzing groups or individuals.

The phrase 'Zoom fatigue' was first popularised during the peak of COVID-19, as millions and millions of 'keyboard-weary adults' (Breslin, 2023) worldwide found themselves working online every day, for several months. For teachers, a great responsibility was placed on them to manage a virtual classroom, support student mental health (digitally) and teach online using the software with the hardware that they had available at home or provided by their employer. There are many headaches with online teaching, not to mention the capability of a person's Wi-Fi signal at home.

The best way in which to improve teaching (instruction) online is to start with a research-based understanding of how people learn. During the pandemic, I found the following piece of research incredibly helpful, and it's still something that guides me today when I work with teachers online. In 'Nine ways to reduce cognitive load in multimedia learning', Mayer and Moreno (2003) propose a theory of learning on the assumption that humans possess separate systems for processing pictorial and verbal material.

Research aims

Mayer and Moreno's (2003) research aims 'to figure out how to use words and pictures to foster meaningful learning' (p. 43). Meaningful learning is defined as 'a deep understanding of the material, which includes attending to important aspects of the presented material, mentally organizing it into a coherent cognitive structure, and integrating it with relevant existing knowledge' (p. 43). The research also evaluates cognitive overload to explain how the learner's intended cognitive processing exceeds the available cognitive capacity.

For those who may be unfamiliar with cognitive load theory (CLT), this is how a learner engages in substantial cognitive processing during the learning experience, but their capacity for processing is severely limited. Mayer and Moreno's paper includes an explanation of how the mind works and a reference to dual coding (Paivio, 1986), plus Sweller's later studies based on his original research on CLT (1988) and Mayer's research (1999, 2002) on the collecting-organising-integrating theory of active learning. These processes all include 'paying attention to the presented material' (Mayer and Moreno, 2003, p. 43).

Five problems with cognitive load

In Mayer and Moreno's (2003) research, five types of cognitive load problems are presented and evaluated:

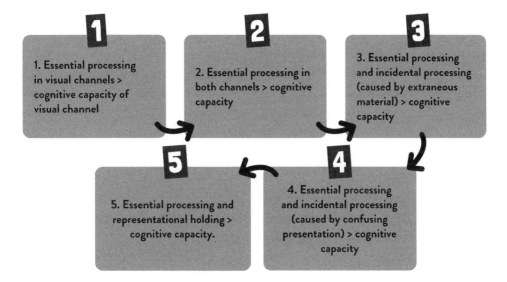

Nine solutions

Across these five evaluations, nine recommendations are presented (Mayer and Moreno, 2003):

1: Offloading

Problem: A student watches a video on 'how lightning works' and is presented with a two-minute animation depicting the steps in lightning formation, along with concurrent on-screen text describing the steps. The text is presented at the bottom of the screen, so the student cannot view the animation while they are reading.

Solution 1: The research recommends presenting words as narration. In this way, the words are processed – at least initially – in the verbal channel, whereas the animation is processed in the visual channel. It's worth reading the full student scenario presented to understand why this is a recommendation. Sometimes the narration text can be phonetically highlighted to help decode the information.

2: Segmenting

Problem: Use the same student problem as above. If the information content is rich and the pace of presentation is fast, learners may not have enough time to engage in the deeper processing of organising the words into a verbal model.

Solution 2: A potential solution is to allow some time between successive segments of the presentation – for example, the presentation is broken down into bite-size segments.

3: Pretraining

Problem: Just as we retrieve information in the classroom, we should also prepare – or 'prime' – students for what is to come. I could demonstrate this simply with the word **'culture'** to prime you for the next chapter in the book. The challenge is how to connect what is to come with what is currently being read (or said) so that it is not redundant information (see 7 below).

Solution 3: 'An alternative technique for reducing cognitive load when both channels are overloaded is pretraining' (Mayer and Moreno, 2003, p. 47) Learners receive prior instruction about the components. The research suggests that 'students performed better on problem-solving transfer tests when the narrated animation was preceded by a short pretraining about the names and behaviours of the components' (p. 47).

4: Weeding

Problem: Suppose a student clicks on the entry for how lightning works in a multimedia encyclopaedia and they receive a narrated animation describing the steps, along with background music or inserted narrated video clips. Adding interesting but extraneous material to narrated animation causes the learner to use limited cognitive resources on incidental processing, leaving less cognitive capacity for essential processing.

Solution 4: In essence, the background music makes things worse! The solution is to reduce extraneous material by using a technique called weeding – a term that I had not come across before. Weeding involves making the narrated animation as concise and coherent as possible, so that the learner will not be primed to engage in incidental processing – engaged as a result of something else! I now remove all background music from my YouTube videos.

5: Signalling

Problem: Very often slide, textbook and worksheet design is too busy. This can be overwhelming for processing information. The font choice, spacing and margin design in this book is all very deliberate.

Solution 5: The research paper suggests that '[w]hen it is not feasible to remove all the embellishments in a... lesson, cognitive load can be reduced by providing cues to the learner about how to select and organise the material – a technique called signaling' (Mayer and Moreno, 2003, p. 48). What we need to do is ensure that the learner does not engage/focus on non-essential facts or graphics. In one study, 'students who received the signaled version of the narrated animation performed better on a subsequent test' (Mautone and Mayer, 2001, Experiment 3, cited in Mayer and Moreno, 2003, p. 48).

6: Aligning words and pictures

Problem: In this situation, a learner is overloaded in one or both channels (auditory and visual). This can easily be created by misaligning words and pictures on a screen or on a worksheet. One study is referenced, explaining that learners tend to read a portion of text and then look at the corresponding portion of the graphic. When the words are far from the corresponding portion of the graphic, the learner is required to use limited cognitive resources to visually scan (Hegarty and Just, 1989, cited in Mayer and Moreno, 2003).

Solution 6: Spatial alignment of words and pictures appears to be a valuable technique for reducing cognitive load. It guides cognitive processing, eliminating the need for incidental processing.

7: Eliminating redundancy

Problem: Another type of cognitive overload occurs when a multimedia presentation consists of simultaneous animation, narration and on-screen text. Therefore, a learner may devote cognitive capacity to processing the on-screen text and reconciling it with the narration – incidental processing reduces the capacity to engage with the essential information.

Solution 7: Another experiment is presented, in which students who learn from non-redundant presentations perform better on problem-solving tests (Mayer et al., 2001, cited in Mayer and Moreno, 2003). Note that weeding involves cutting interesting but irrelevant material, whereas eliminating redundancy involves cutting any unneeded duplication of essential material.

8. Synchronising

Problem: One or both channels are overloaded when the learner attempts to engage in both essential processing (selecting, organising) and processing material (holding visual/verbal material in working memory). When no animation is presented, students learn better from a presentation of narration and on-screen text (verbal redundancy).

Solution 8: A straightforward solution is to synchronise the presentation of visual and auditory material. This will minimise cognitive load. This should be no different to how we use questioning in a classroom, and in an online context. The question must be relevant to the learning, and introduced at the right time.

9: Individualising

Problem: It is important for teachers to help 'learners possess skill in holding mental representations in memory' (Mayer and Moreno, 2003, p. 50). With all the other difficulties that a teacher may face, this is a real challenge. A research paper quoted discovered that high spatial learners performed much better on tests from simultaneous presentation, whereas low spatial learners performed at a lower level (Mayer and Sims, 1994, cited in Mayer and Moreno, 2003, p.50).

Solution 9: Spatial ability effect is recommended, matching high-quality multimedia materials with high spatial learners as a useful technique for reducing cognitive load. There is no reference to what the solution is for learners with low spatial ability.

Recommendations for teachers

How can teachers make learning easier to access? There are some immediate fixes that teachers can try. The challenge is that, with limited resources and time, sticking all the information onto one online worksheet, rather than consciously dividing the information into four or five different documents to present as and when needed, is a real challenge for teachers. The researchers conclude that 'concise narrated animation fostered meaningful learning without creating cognitive overload' (Mayer and Moreno, 2003, p. 51).

PRACTICAL IDEA

Online questioning and software

Here are the nine principles (Mayer and Moreno, 2010) for working more effectively online in the virtual classroom:

1. offloading

2. segmenting

3. pretraining; prior instruction

4. weeding

5. signalling

6. aligning words and pictures to guide processing

7. eliminating redundancy

8. synchronising visual and auditory information

9. individualising; match the material to the learners.

How have teachers adapted to teaching online, particularly from a questioning perspective? We need to consider the following:

1. Will the lesson be synchronous? Synchronous lessons are when the teacher and students are online at the same time, either in person or through video conferencing, and the lesson is conducted in real time.

2. Will the lesson be asynchronous? Asynchronous lessons are when the teacher and students are not online at the same time, and the lesson is conducted through a pre-recorded video or other material that can be accessed at any time.

3. How old are the students?

4. What do the students know?

5. What's been taught so far?

6. What time of day is it?

7. How long is the lesson?

8. What technology is being used and how is it being received?
Zoom, Microsoft Teams, Google Meet, etc.)

9. What are the advantages or disadvantages of the technology, and how will this hinder or support the teaching and learning process?

10. Are students working alone or sharing a device?

All these contextual factors will provide you with many different possibilities.

In *Lessons from Lockdown: The Educational Legacy of COVID-19* (2021), Tony Breslin assesses the educational legacy of the pandemic and the potential that it offers for reframing how we 'do' schooling. The book is directed at policymakers and considers how decisions were made during the time of crisis and how this evolving pandemic was received on the front line, by parents and students too. There is a reference to parental engagement and the experience of learning at home, and this is something worth considering in the context of questioning and in an online environment for the future.

> **'Like the virus itself, this empathy (a two-way interaction) emerges from an intrusion on both sides into the lives of teachers and students; the poverty that some of the young people and their families contend with on a daily basis is stripped bare.'**
> **(Breslin, 2021)**

A key question is how to create an engaging and effective questioning approach to online teaching. One way of doing this is to use interactive teaching models, such as the flipped classroom, which encourages student-led teaching and learning, and allows students to take more ownership of their learning. This could be done by using tools such as Google Classroom or Kahoot!, which allow teachers to set up quizzes or activities for students to complete on their own. This increases student engagement and encourages active learning. However, student led learning must be considered carefully in the context of what students already know, what they're being asked to do, and the resources available to them. Additionally, online tools such as Mentimeter or Socrative enable teachers to create interactive questionnaires that allow students to respond in real time. There are so many brilliant online pieces of software. A new resource, which is simply phenomenal, is Primary Quiz!

Whichever tools and approaches are used, teachers should help to engage all students, assess the current level of understanding and adjust the lesson accordingly. Additionally, teachers can use chat functions or discussion boards to allow students to ask questions and express their views in a safe and supportive environment. Teachers can do this by setting ground rules at the start of the lesson, managing the traffic content and flow, and encouraging students to be conscious of procedures and online protocols.

Scan this QR code to find out about 9 ways you can reduce cognitive load.

1. Consider all the contextual factors, such as the technology used, whether students are working alone and whether or not the lesson is synchronous, when designing your online teaching.

2. Interactive teaching models like the flipped classroom enable students to take ownership of their learning.

3. Chat functions and discussion boards can encourage engagement from all students.

WORKED EXAMPLE

In order to effectively teach in an online environment, teachers should focus on research-based learning theory to reduce cognitive load and create engaging materials. This includes strategies such as offloading, segmenting, pretraining, weeding, signalling, aligning words and pictures, eliminating redundancy, synchronising and individualising.

For example, a teacher could create an interactive quiz using a tool like Kahoot! or Mentimeter to provide students with pretraining on the content before engaging with the material. This reduces cognitive load by allowing the students to focus on the essential information and helps them to better organise the material. Additionally, the teacher could use chat functions or discussion boards to allow students to ask questions, express their views and stay engaged with the lesson.

Considering questioning specifically, here is an online scenario. The following is a scripted role play of a teacher teaching a lesson online using Zoom, with a group of 30 students logged into their own devices remotely. The lesson is for 60 minutes, and the topic is teaching fractions to Year 6 students. The teacher can assign students with polls, quizzes and QR codes to watch videos. When called for a demonstration, the teacher can allow the students to annotate an online whiteboard in group work situations to show their calculations on the screen to the whole class.

Teacher: 'Good morning everyone, I'm so glad you could join us today. We're going to be learning about improper fractions, recapping on proper fractions shared in our last lesson. So, let's get started. To start off, I'd like to ask each of you to tell me what you know about improper fractions.'

Students: *(Various responses in the chat box.)*

Teacher: 'Alright, now let's get into the nitty-gritty. To help me to explain how to convert improper fractions into mixed numbers, I'm going to use a few examples. I'm going to ask you to watch this video with me.' *(Insert link here.)*

Teacher: 'Now, let's take a few minutes to practise what we have learned. I'm going to assign you a poll with a few simple questions. Go ahead and try to answer the questions.' *(After the poll has been completed, the teacher can review the results with the class.)*

Teacher: 'OK, let's review the results. It looks like *[review the results here]*. Now, I'd like to assign each of you a few questions to work on. Watch me demonstrate a problem and possible solution. I'll give you 15 minutes to work on them. Go ahead and use the whiteboard to show your calculations.'

Using ABC (Agree, Build, Challenge)

This example shows how the teacher can use the ABC questioning strategy in the above online context. The premise of this book is that each questioning idea builds upon the previous technique, so the challenge aspect is added for you as a practitioner. By doing so to the point of automaticity, you can reduce your workload.

Teacher: 'Now Year 6, can anyone tell me how fractions can be used in everyday life?' *(Agree)*

Student 1: 'Proper fractions are like a part of a whole number. So, if you have a number like 3/4, it means 3 out of 4 parts.' *(Build)*

Teacher: 'Very good, that's correct! Now can anyone give me an example of how fractions can be used in real life?' *(Challenge)*

Student 2: 'We can use fractions to measure things like ingredients when baking, or to divide up a pizza into equal parts.' *(Agree)*

Teacher: 'That's right, fractions are used all the time in everyday life. Now let's take a look at some examples. I'm going to assign a poll to your devices so you can answer questions as we go along. First, I'm going to show you an example of a fraction. Can anyone tell me what this fraction is?' *(Shows 3/4 on the screen.) (Build)*

Student 3: 'That's 3/4.' *(Agree)*

Teacher: 'Excellent, so we can see that 3/4 is a fraction. Now, I would like you all to explain why knowing how to simplify fractions is useful? Add your answer to the following document. *(URL link shared by teacher) (Challenge)*

TEMPLATE

ABC

Scan the QR code to learn more about how to use the ABC questioning technique in the classroom from Jonathan Sandling.

Use this template to plan ahead your ABC methodology for a future lesson.

Stage	Action
1	Introduce the topic with a broad question that encourages students to share their existing knowledge and opinions. (AGREE)
2	Acknowledge and build upon students' responses by summarising and expanding upon their ideas. (BUILD)
3	Challenge students to think more deeply about the topic by asking a follow-up question that requires analysis or evaluation of their own or others' ideas. (CHALLENGE)
4	Provide examples or demonstrations to illustrate key concepts and help students visualise or understand the topic. (BUILD)
5	Ask students to explain or apply what they've learned by posing a question or problem that requires them to use their new knowledge. (CHALLENGE)
6	Encourage students to reflect on their learning by asking them to share what they found challenging or interesting, and what they've learned from the activity. (AGREE)

CHAPTER 7
DEVELOPING QUESTIONING CULTURE

Building a questioning culture

In this chapter, I will look at how a **questioning culture** can be developed across an entire school, and how this questioning culture can enhance teachers' performance and the performance of people with whom they work – students, parents and governors – as well as how it can enhance the vision and values of the organisation. The key questioning technique shared in this chapter is the **question matrix**. This is a fabulous tool, and something that I have used for almost 15 years.

How can schools build a questioning culture in all classrooms and facilitate teachers' ability to do so? This question also applies to staff culture, where effective questioning and listening permeate meetings, lesson observations and line management teams. To exemplify a questioning culture, it is interesting to look at forest schools, alternative provisions and outdoor education settings. These settings often have inspiring educational initiatives carried out by passionate and committed educators who understand the importance of creativity, collaboration and innovation in teaching and learning.

Two incredible places that I have visited were a forest school in Akrotiri, Cyprus and a new Early Years facility in Amman, Jordan. Both outdoor learning spaces were filled with natural materials and resources, allowing children to explore, discover and create in a safe and stimulating environment. Through activities such as building shelters, exploring the natural world and creating art, I saw how the students were engaged in learning and expressed their creativity. However, this 'learning' was not designed by chance.

Some critics of 'discovery learning' or 'play' argue that unstructured teaching – at least to the untrained eye – does more harm than good when developing students' (domain-specific) knowledge. In the UK, I have visited alternative provisions and special educational needs schools, where I have been inspired by the dedication of the teachers, the resources available and the level of support and understanding for the children and their families. I have seen how these settings can be a place of safety, growth and learning for children at the most critical stage of their schooling. I have been amazed by the determination and depth of knowledge of those teachers working in the Early Years sector. This leads me to pose two key questions:

1. How does questioning in the Early Years classroom facilitate learning?

2. How does 'guided play' support early development and learning?

It is difficult to draw robust conclusions for these two questions. In their research, Skene et al. (2022) ask, 'Can guidance during play enhance children's learning and development in an educational context?' Recent policy developments in the USA and UK have moved towards a greater academic focus, which has triggered a debate about the role of play-based learning in Early Years and primary school settings. Skene et al.'s research study compares direct instruction against guided play to support 'free play' in children's learning and development.

Research Aims

The researchers conducted a randomised controlled trial, where students were assigned by chance to either an intervention group or a control group, alongside non-randomised control trials involving students being exposed to both conditions. Thirty-nine studies were reviewed and participants were children (n = 3,893) generally aged from one to eight years, regardless of gender, ethnicity, ability or social-economic status. In total, 49.8 per cent were girls, 41 per cent were White, 28 per cent were African American/Black and 19 per cent were Hispanic. After data extraction, findings were examined quantitatively and qualitatively.

The concept of guided play has three essential elements that co-create an ideal environment for learning:

3.

The teacher should demonstrate adaptability in using various guidance techniques, including questions and prompts.

1.

When arranging a guided play, it is important for the teacher guiding the experience to have well-defined learning objectives.

2.

The play activity or interaction should grant students a certain level of autonomy and the *ability to make choices. (*age-dependent)

(Skene et al., 2022, p. 1163)

> '… meta-analyses identified significant evidence for guided play having a greater positive effect than direct instruction on early maths skills, shape knowledge, and task switching, and a positive effect than free play on spatial vocabulary.'
> (Skene et al., 2022, p. 1173)

Note that differences are not identified for other numeracy, executive function, literacy or socio-emotional outcomes, such as expressive vocabulary, shape knowledge or prosocial behaviour (Skene et al., 2022). Interestingly, in single studies, guided play when compared to direct instruction in all outcome domains is identified to have a greater positive effect than free play (Skene et al., 2022). This will be reassuring to all teachers working in Early Years and primary school settings, and will provide food for thought for policymakers considering baseline tests that will be used in Reception (and how they can measure academic progress which does not value the cognitive benefits of guided play).

Given the busy nature of school life, how can schools engineer guided play into their curriculum time? As with all research, there are limitations and bias within the findings. 'What works, under what conditions?' is a question that all teachers must ask when accessing research recommendations, but we should also ask 'why' and 'how'. An understanding of the state of the evidence regarding the effectiveness of play-based learning is needed to inform decisions about teacher education and professional development. In Skene et al.'s review of the literature, it suggests that guided play is beneficial for children's learning and development in an educational context. Whilst this will come as no surprise for Early Years or primary teacher practitioners, how do we raise the status of what teachers do in the early years of school life with policymakers?

So, how do teachers pose effective questions to guide learning in a primary context, and what techniques do they use? Here are five practical tips:

1. Use open-ended questions and prompts to encourage critical thinking, creativity and problem-solving skills.

2. Provide structured opportunities for guided play to develop early attitudes and approaches to learning.

3. Integrate guided play into existing lessons and activities.

4. Use a variety of questioning techniques to guide learning, and make learning concrete and engaging.

5. Consider the context and multiple sources of evidence when accessing research recommendations, and reflect on and adjust your approach as needed.

EXPLAINER

How do you build a questioning culture in a school?

In this chapter, I have selected the **question matrix** as the perfect idea to demonstrate how a teacher, or a group of teachers could build a questioning culture.

A questioning culture is one in which the school community encourages and values questioning, critical thinking and intellectual curiosity. 'If you want to accelerate learning in any endeavour, you concentrate on the group' (Hargreaves and Fullan, 2012, p. 14); it should be fostered in all aspects of school life, from the classroom to extra-curricular activities to school policies and adult behaviours, and in role players like parents or community members.

'Implementation science is a universal strategy to ensure that programmes make sustainable positive differences.' (Moir, 2018, p. 7) Introducing and embedding any ideas can take many years. It is also worth defining 'culture' and what this looks like on the ground: 'the shared beliefs, values, customs, behaviours' (Hargreaves and Fullan, 2012) that characterise a school or community. 'Culture' is the way in which things get done in a particular context. From my work with schools all over the world, 'culture' is often one of the biggest projects school leaders work with on an annual basis.

In 'The design and validation of the enabling conditions for collective teacher efficacy scale' by Donohoo et al. (2020), researchers asked whether they could measure the antecedents (conditions) of collective teacher efficacy (CTE). It's worth here defining CTE and efficacy:

1. CTE is a marker for improved student learning, particularly shared among teachers in a school.

2. Efficacy means: The ability to produce a desired or intended result.

The research highlights:

1. school processes that have a strong influence on prior achievement

2. a supportive environment where teachers can contribute

3. an environment where teachers can interact with one another

4. how 'contextual variables [also] add power to explanations of [CTE]' (Donohoo et al., 2020, p. 149).

So, what does this mean for teachers?

1. **Advanced teacher influence:** Teachers are trusted to make important decisions. Not 'Where do you want the photocopier?' but key decisions on the timing of the school day, uniform, values etc.

2. **Assessment as feedback:** Common conceptions of progress are developed.

3. **Cohesion:** Beliefs about effective instruction, approaches and assessment are shared. Teachers are aware of what others are doing in the classroom.

4. **Goal consensus:** Goals are established/agreed by everyone –collaborative CPD (continuous professional development).

5. **Responsiveness:** Support staff help teachers to carry out their duties and school leaders show concern for the staff and protect them. Interventions are in place to ensure high levels of success for all students, including tracking and monitoring.

How many of the above do you think your school can confidently say they achieve? School leadership can use this research to help to inform practice and instil a greater sense of collective efficacy among the teachers in a school, but this means that there needs to be a 'willingness to invest the time and energy required to attain educational goals and results in greater effort' (Donohoo et al., 2020, p. 147).

The **first step** in building a questioning culture is to create an environment that is welcoming and encouraging. This includes providing students with opportunities to ask questions, encouraging teachers to ask questions in their classrooms and rewarding students for their inquisitiveness. It also means providing teachers with resources and materials that foster an atmosphere of inquiry and critical thinking.

The **second step** is important in ensuring that students are taught the skills for questioning. This includes teaching them to ask open-ended and probing questions, to think critically, to form their own opinions and to engage in meaningful dialogue. Earlier chapters of this book have provided practical ways of doing this.

The **final step** is ensuring that the school provides an atmosphere of trust and safety. This means that students feel comfortable asking questions and engaging in critical thinking, without fear of ridicule or punishment. It also means that teachers are receptive to student questions and are willing to engage in dialogue about the topics being discussed.

Building a questioning culture in a school requires a collective effort from all members of the school community. It requires teachers, school leaders and parents to work together to provide the resources and environment needed to foster a questioning culture. With commitment and dedication, a school can create a culture of questioning and critical thinking.

One of the many schools I know of that does this well is **Staffordshire University Academy** in Cannock, England. This school has totally revamped the conduct of performance management, flipping the traditional model where targets are imposed on teachers by their line managers, instead opting for a research-informed inquiry question, designed by the teacher – and support staff, I hasten to add – and threaded through professional development to a whole-staff celebration at the end of the academic year.

With permission, I have shared an anonymised example of what all schools should aspire to via the QR code. I believe this is one document ALL schools should be producing.

This school is a great example of schools that have built a culture of questioning and critical thinking.

In keeping with their vision to drive staff culture, autonomy and engagement with research, Staffordshire University Academy has just published this year's evidence-informed projects – their 5th year of documenting an alternative to performance management – which I'm pleased to share with you exclusively. Scan the QR code for direct access.

PRACTICAL IDEA

The question matrix

The question matrix on the page opposite uses Socratic questioning, which has a six-step process:

1. clarify

2. challenge assumption

3. evidence for an argument

4. gather viewpoints and perspectives

5. predict implications and consequences

6. question the question.

It is one of the most popular resource downloads on my website and I have been sharing it online for almost a decade. I'm still surprised that very few staff have ever come across it, which reminds me that I should always share great teaching ideas to ensure everyone benefits from tried-and-tested resources that have a big impact on teaching and learning. The principle of using the matrix evolved from the original Bloom's taxonomy thinking. It requires students to answer questions at each level. The aim is to help students to understand a concept, think critically and apply their knowledge.

The six steps of the question matrix are as follows:

1. Knowledge and comprehension: Questions are designed to test a student's knowledge and understanding of a given topic.

2. Application: Questions are designed to test a student's ability to apply their knowledge and understanding of the given topic.

3. Analysis: Questions are designed to analyse a student's ability to break down a concept into its component parts.

4. Synthesis: Questions are designed to assess a student's ability to combine ideas and form new ones.

5. Evaluation: Questions are designed to evaluate a student's ability to make judgements and draw conclusions based on evidence.

QUESTION MATRIX	IS? DOES? Present	HAS? DID? WAS? Past	CAN? Possibility	SHOULD? Opinion	WOULD? COULD? Probability	WILL? Prediction	MIGHT? Imagination
WHAT? Event							
WHERE? Place							
WHEN? Time							
WHICH? Choice							
WHO? Person							
WHY? Reason							
HOW? Meaning							

AS SCHEMATIC KNOWLEDGE STRENGTHENS, THE QUESTION FORMAT (FROM TOP-LEFT TO BOTTOM-RIGHT) SUPPORTS THE DEVELOPMENT OF METACOGNITION.

6. Creativity: Questions are designed to assess a student's ability to think outside the box and come up with creative solutions.

The beauty of the resource is that it is a great tool for teachers to use on their slide decks, in handouts for their students and in live displays on classroom walls, where students can pin questions into various segments. Where I have seen it work really well is when teachers facilitate students to use the resource within a variety of techniques, as outlined below:

1. a blank template, evolving over time as students enter one or two questions each lesson

2. a script for teaching assistants to use alongside vulnerable students

3. a working wall or corridor display

4. a prompt for whole-school assembly

5. an acetate periscope for live displays (cut out the middle area).

Scan the QR code to see a video display of the acetate periscope.

TOOLKIT TIPS

1. Start with simple questions and move on to more complex ideas.

2. Initial questions should test students' knowledge and understanding and their ability to apply this.

3. Later questions should encourage students to break down and combine ideas.

4. Final questions should probe students' creativity and ability to draw conclusions.

WORKED EXAMPLE

Some example questions to ask teaching and support staff can be used not only to model effective questions, but also to model the development of a high-performing culture.

1. Does your site manager engage with appraisal?

2. Do your support staff engage with professional development?

3. Do your support staff get the same diet of CPD as the teaching staff?

4. Do all your members of staff participate in education research?

5. Are your appraisal targets set from above or curated bottom-up?

6. Other than the traditional training days, do all your staff have regular CPD throughout the year?

7. Do you have a process for nurturing and developing your own talent?

8. Do your staff feel like they are part of a community or just a cog in a machine?

9. Do you have a process for dealing with underperforming staff?

10. How can the minutiae of lesson observation be separated from your capability procedures?

11. Does your school still grade lessons?

12. Is there an established coaching culture?

13. Is there a dedicated teaching and learning team?

14. Do all staff receive coaching?

15. Is there a wellbeing policy?

16. Is there a wellbeing budget and staff lead?

17. Does your school protect 0.1 per cent of its overall budget for staff professional development?

18. Does your school grade teacher appraisal?

19. Do you have a way of celebrating the great work that your staff do?

20. Is your headteacher present at all CPD events?

TEMPLATE

Question matrix

This is probably one of the most powerful resources I can share with you. You can use this copy of the Question Matrix table in several ways:

1. displayed on the board at the front of class; students to come up to the board and place sticky notes with questions/swap the sticky notes with questions

2. add an image; use as a lesson prompt for discussions

3. cut out the middle and add acetate; use as a life modelling periscope

4. provide matrix to a teaching assistant to use alongside a student they are working with as a way to develop metacognitive thinking.

QUESTION MATRIX	IS? DOES? Present	HAS? DID? WAS? Past	CAN? Possibility	SHOULD? Opinion	WOULD? COULD? Probability	WILL? Prediction	MIGHT? Imagination
WHAT? Event							
WHERE? Place							
WHEN? Time							
WHICH? Choice							
WHO? Person							
WHY? Reason							
HOW? Meaning							

CHAPTER 8
EFFECTIVE CPD

CPD questioning

In this chapter, I will explore the research on **effective professional development** and how it can be used to create a questioning culture in schools, to help teachers to thrive in their day-to-day work. The key questioning technique shared in this chapter is **EEAA – elaborate, evidence, arguments for, arguments against** – which is a useful framework for developing thinking in others and improving performance, and a fabulous classroom strategy. I will also provide a practical idea for using this technique in the classroom, as well as sharing case studies from Investors in People to demonstrate how other organisations have successfully implemented this strategy. Finally, I will explore how effective feedback, adequate resources and an ongoing commitment from the school are all essential for successful professional development of its workforce.

Where would you start if you wanted to build a culture of effective questioning across a school organisation? What would the teacher training look like? How often would you need to revisit strategies and provide teachers with time to practise, and where, when and how would you bring them together to share what they are doing in the classrooms?

The more challenging question is: how does a school design an effective teacher training programme?

EXPLAINER

To begin with, we should look at some research to identify the hallmarks of effective professional development, such as that of the Education Endowment Foundation or Evidence Based Education, both of which offer some excellent insights into professional development. The practical technique, **Explain, Evidence, Arguments for and Against (EEAA)** is the technique suggested in this section for teachers to use with their students. I believe the same idea could apply for teachers as critical consumers of education research and professional development. I also want to look at other sectors and learn how businesses and other industries design effective induction – sometimes called onboarding – and perhaps find some organisations that have excellent retention rates. The challenge is to translate these ways of working to teachers working with young students who may challenge our best intentions.

Effective professional development requires the use of regular and targeted feedback. Feedback is an essential part of the learning process, as it allows everyone to reflect on their performance, make necessary improvements and receive recognition for their efforts. Regular feedback encourages people to review their progress and identify areas for development. It also helps to create a culture of continuous learning and improvement.

The Great Teaching Toolkit, published by Evidence Based Education (Coe et al., 2020), is a comprehensive peer-reviewed publication that offers an evidence review route map for all teachers. It asks 'What are your best bets in terms of making the most difference to your students?'. The publication offers 17 elements within four components and is a useful document to use in a teacher's professional development. I was privileged enough to be asked to help peer-review the document prior to publication.

TABLE: 17 ELEMENTS

Source: Evidence Based Education

Components	Elements					
1. Understanding the content	1. Having a deep and fluent knowledge	2. Knowledge of the requirements of curriculum sequencing	3. Knowledge of relevant curriculum tasks, assessments and activities	4. Knowledge of common student strategies		
2. Creating a supportive environment	1. Promoting interactions and relationships with all students	2. Promoting a positive climate	3. Promoting motivation through feelings of competence, autonomy and relatedness	4. Creating a climate of high expectations, with high challenge and high trust		
3. Maximising the opportunity to learn	1. Managing time and resources efficiently in the classroom	2. Rules, expectations and consequences for behaviour are explicit, clear and consistently applied	3. Preventing, anticipating and responding to potentially disruptive incidents			
4. Activating hard thinking	1. Structuring: giving students on an appropriate sequence of learning tasks	2. Explaining: presenting and communicating new ideas clearly	3. Questioning: using questions and dialogue to promote elaboration and connected, flexible thinking	4. Interacting: responding appropriately to feedback from students about their thinking	5. Embedding: giving students tasks that embed and reinforce learning; requiring them to practise	6. Activating: helping students to plan, regulate and monitor their own learning

The top three rows in the table are what all new teachers need to learn and master. No matter how experienced a teacher is, they won't initially master all 11 elements; they are developed over the course of a teaching year and across the first few years of teaching. Once understanding content, creating supportive learning environments and managing opportunities to learn are securely in place, all teachers can focus on their pedagogical strategies, which, in turn, need constant refining to help 'activate hard thinking'.

The challenge for our leadership teams is, how do they get the best performance out of their colleagues? Training may be limited, budgets may be low and time, accountability and stress can make wanting to be the best that you can be a very difficult thing to achieve. The answer is to ensure that those in leadership positions have the right training, support and resources to help them to manage the pressures of their roles. This includes making sure that they have access to the right professional development, access to the support and resources that they need and the opportunity to take on new challenges. Additionally, it is important to ensure a culture of accountability, and leaders should be held to the same standards as their colleagues. This will help to create a culture of excellence and ensure that everyone is striving to be the best that they can be.

It is essential to ensure that the organisation and its leadership team have the right systems to make sure that everyone is working to their full potential. This includes creating clear goals, setting expectations and monitoring progress. When everyone is working towards the same goal, it is much easier to achieve success.

Finally, effective professional development requires an ongoing commitment from both the teachers and the school. This commitment is essential for the development to be successful, and should include adequate time for collaboration and planning, as well as ongoing professional development opportunities. In addition, it should include an evaluation process to ensure that the development is meeting the desired outcomes.

Here are some simple, yet powerful questions you can ask to determine the culture and high performance of employers you might work with:

- Which organisations provide effective feedback on employee performance and how does this impact motivation, retention and productivity?

- How does the organisation succession plan for:
  - a) recruitment
  - b) diversity, quality and inclusion
  - c) gender pay
  - d) risk assessment (e.g. pandemic) or
  - e) technology (e.g. artificial intelligence, misinformation and disinformation)?
- Which organisations organise training effectively, with limited time and budgets?
- Which organisations demonstrate an ongoing commitment to their workforce?

Some of the world's best organisations have a few key things in common:

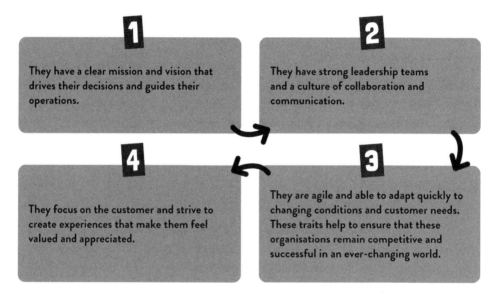

1
They have a clear mission and vision that drives their decisions and guides their operations.

2
They have strong leadership teams and a culture of collaboration and communication.

4
They focus on the customer and strive to create experiences that make them feel valued and appreciated.

3
They are agile and able to adapt quickly to changing conditions and customer needs. These traits help to ensure that these organisations remain competitive and successful in an ever-changing world.

Investors in People (IIP) is an international standard for people management. It is owned by the UK government and provides a framework to help organisations improve their performance through people. The standard is split into nine areas, which cover everything from planning and leading, to supporting and developing people. Organisations are assessed against the standard and awarded a level of accreditation based on their performance. This accreditation is nationally recognised and can be used to demonstrate an organisation's commitment to its people.

Here are two case study examples from IIP that represent excellent professional development.

1. The homeless charity, St Petrocs in Cornwall, England, 'delivers a range of services to an extremely vulnerable group of people in challenging circumstances' (IIP, no date). The company was recognised for its unwavering commitment to people and culture.

2. Harrison Spinks (www.harrisonspinks.co.uk) is a luxury, family-run bedmaker that employs over 700 people. It is recognised for the people within the organisation that make the difference between a good-performing company and a worldwide leading company.

But the questions remain, what are they doing to build a happy organisation? What does the training look like?

PRACTICAL IDEA

The EEAA strategy

A school needs to clearly define what they consider to be effective questioning and what the purpose of that questioning should be – for example, to promote critical thinking and problem-solving, encourage collaboration and further student understanding. Once this has been established, the school would need to design a comprehensive teacher training programme that encompasses different types of questioning techniques and strategies and how to use these in the classroom. The teacher training programme should also provide ample opportunities to practise the skills that the trainees have learned in their training. Teachers could practise asking questions in their classrooms and then discuss their experiences in a group setting.

The school could also provide teachers with feedback on their progress from other teachers or the school leadership. This feedback could help teachers to adjust their strategies to make them more effective. This approach can, however, be very mixed. Finally, I would suggest that the school provides teachers with regular opportunities to come together and share their experiences. It could be done through professional development sessions, where teachers could share their successes and failures using questioning techniques. This could create a culture of effective questioning and help to identify areas where teachers need additional support. Overall, effective professional development requires a combination of regular and targeted feedback, adequate resources and support, and an ongoing commitment from both teachers and the school.

One of my doctoral colleagues at Cambridge University, Jonathan Sandling, has kindly shared his question techniques for teachers to help them ask better questions. 'EEAA is a strategy that all teachers can use in the lessons to generate more discussion and debate.' (Sandling, 2021)

Elaborate

When students reply to a question, a simple fix for all teachers is simply to ask students to elaborate on their answer. For readers familiar with the research on study skills – see Dunlosky et al. (2013) – asking students to be able to explain 'why' is equipping students to think metacognitively,

particularly relevant when students are providing an opinion in response to a student question.

Evidence

Following a student's answer, ask, 'What do you mean by this?' or 'Why is this important?'. Alternatively, ask them to provide some concrete evidence. It is helpful to triangulate information and sources of evidence.

Arguments for and against

Here are some example prompts that a teacher might use to help a student to develop an **argument for** a particular topic or issue:

1. What evidence can you find to support your position on a particular issue?

2. What are the benefits of taking this position, and how do they outweigh the costs?

3. What are the main reasons why someone might disagree with your position, and how can you respond to these counter arguments effectively?

4. How does your position on this issue align with your personal values and beliefs?

5. Give me some examples of other people that share your position on this issue, and how they have been successful in promoting their ideas.

6. How might your position on this issue affect different groups of people, and what steps can be taken to address any potential negative consequences?

7. How does this issue relate to larger societal trends or movements, and what role can your position play in promoting positive change?

8. What are some potential alternatives to your position, and how do they compare in terms of effectiveness, feasibility and ethics?

These prompts can help students to think critically about their position on a particular issue and develop a well-supported argument that can be persuasive to others.

A teacher can flip these questions when developing **arguments against** a topic. For example, 'What **conflicting** evidence can you find to **challenge** someone's views of XYZ?'

'Pose, pause, pounce, bounce' (see Chapter 1) is a great methodology to employ when hosting classroom debates alongside these techniques. A teacher can manage classroom discussions in developing arguments for and against by using 'posing' or 'bouncing' to **orchestrate** conversations between students who want to elaborate on their answers and views.

1. Looking at successful non-education organisations can give you ideas for creating a happy ethos and effective training in a school context.

2. Just like when teaching students, a teacher training programme should encompass a range of questioning techniques and strategies.

3. Be sure to provide teachers with ample opportunities to come together and share and discuss their experiences.

4. Asking students to elaborate and to provide evidence and arguments for and against is a great technique to encourage them to think critically and generate debate.

WORKED EXAMPLE

Google is a multi-billion-pound technology company that offers a range of individualised training programmes and resources for its employees, including Google University, career development programmes and a '20 per cent time' policy that allows employees to work on projects outside of their usual job responsibilities. Google's approach to professional development is highly focused on individual ownership and development, as well as a culture of feedback and collaboration.

A good example of Google's approach to professional development is their 'Googler-to-Googler', (G2G) programme – a volunteer peer-to-peer learning initiative – that encourages Google employees to share their knowledge, skills and expertise with one another through informal training sessions, workshops and presentations. Empowering people to take control of their own learning nurtures loyal employees, and heightens their autonomy and productivity.

High Tech High, a network of public charter schools in San Diego, California, is highly innovative. The schools place a strong emphasis on professional development for teachers, which includes collaborative planning time, ongoing feedback and coaching. Professional development is highly collaborative and teacher-led, and values ongoing learning and growth for both students and teachers. I know that many schools have this philosophy across the UK, but in the context of the UK, the conditions in which teachers work, the lack of professional development (defined by lack of time) results in one of the lowest investments for our teaching profession when compared to other OECD countries.

Both Google and High Tech High demonstrate a commitment to professional development as a key part of their success. Lots of stand-alone schools here in the UK also share this commitment, and while Google's approach is unique, with an enormous pool of financial resources, alongside High Tech High (and possibly a school near you), there is a strong emphasis on ongoing feedback and growth. What 'good' looks like in terms of effective professional development includes coaching and autonomous performance management, with a focus on innovation, collaboration and a commitment to ongoing learning and development.

TEMPLATE

EEAA

Use the following template to plan how you will use EEAA when planning lessons. I have also included the pose, pause, pounce, bounce questioning technique to add more value.

Stage	Teacher Action	Student Response
1	Elaborate e.g. Could you explain to me why you have chosen A instead of B?	
2	Evidence e.g. Could you give me one source of primary and one source of secondary evidence?	
3	Arguments for e.g. Give me one example to justify your argument.	
4	Arguments against e.g. Could you find one person who disagrees with you, who can also provide an argument against XYZ?	
5	Pose, pause, pounce, bounce e.g. Could you summarise what you have said, but say it again in another way? (followed by a long pause)	

CHAPTER 9
LEADERSHIP QUESTIONING

Forming better working relationships

In this chapter, I explain how questioning and feedback methods help teachers to form **better working relationships**. This can be achieved through **critical friendship,** the **tuning protocol** and the use of **structured procedures**.

- **Critical friendship** involves a dialogue between colleagues that helps to foster understanding and shared meaning.

- The **tuning protocol** helps to improve individual performance through the use of data and collaboration between teachers and leaders.

- **Structured procedures** can help to ensure equitable participation during instruction, allowing people to use the language with which they are most comfortable.

All of these methods can help to foster better working relationships, improved performance and increased morale. We will also look at the feedback methods that schools can use to improve teachers' working relationships in the following ways:

- communicating objectives, strategies and expectations clearly

- listening to team members and being open to feedback and ideas

- demonstrating emotional intelligence

- inspiring team members and recognising when they may be overwhelmed.

'The power of protocols for equity' (Hammond, 2020), reveals insights into classroom visits and 'who is doing most of the talking during instruction'. The message is that when school leaders observe teachers, it's important that trust is established and maintained.

To read 'The power of protocols for equity' (Hammond, 2020), scan this QR code

EXPLAINER

How can teachers work better with colleagues?

In the book *Liminal Leadership*, Tierney (2016) highlights liminality within the scientific study of human behaviour (anthropology). Liminality is when people no longer hold their status in their day-to-day life, as they have begun transitioning to another status as a result of a new endeavour. For example, I may be your headteacher at work, but as soon as I start a master's degree course with a group of strangers, I no longer hold that positional status. I become a peer on a similar journey with others, regardless of whether or not they are a teacher, a headteacher or someone in another profession. We begin a new journey together on a common standing.

If we now frame this in the context of working together in a school, there are a variety of background distractions, such as deadlines and past performance. An effective way to use the **tuning protocol** is to work with people that you know to develop critical friendships and improve performance (Storey and Wang, 2016; Appleby, 1998; Cushman, 1998; Bambino, 2002).

In 'Critical friendship, dialogue and learning, in the context of leadership for learning' (Swaffield, 2008), the research examined the commonalities and differences in how critical friendship operated in seven countries.

> **'At the core of critical friendship is dialogue, a very particular form of conversation involving the exchange of ideas and the search for shared meaning and common understanding.'**
> **(Swaffield, 2008, p. 328)**

Think about your professional colleagues:

1. Do they listen to each other without interruption?

2. Do they respect each other's viewpoints or do they pontificate?

3. Do they accept the discipline of collective problem-solving?

4. Do they stick to the topic in hand?

5. Is disbelief suspended?

6. Does the discussion go round in circles?

7. Do the participants have the skills required by the process?

Swaffield (2008) concluded that at a leadership level, critical friendship is a way of developing relationships, moving away from 'fostering dialogue to reflecting critically on the very nature of dialogic learning and the conditions that support and enhance it'.

Looking more carefully at the tuning protocol in schools, 'Trust in teacher conversations' (Man Loon, 2018) chose to research the single topic of 'trust' in the context of a teacher's conversation in professional learning, with trust defined as consisting of five facets:

1. benevolence (expressed towards others; fairness; confidentiality)

2. reliability (perceiving trust; consistency; from peers)

3. competence (capability; qualification)

4. honesty (authenticity; accepting responsibility; avoiding manipulation)

5. openness (personal information; although too much can counter trust).

The research reported that: 'Initially, I assumed that teachers' trust was transactional... When many teachers build trust... a school is positioned to have greater trust as a whole' (Man Loon, 2018, p. 130). The researcher understood the theory of trust as being tangible. If you ask any teacher what they want the most (other than better teacher pay and good student behaviour), being **trusted** is their number one need.

The research goes on to provide an overview of the literature on the **fine-tuning protocol** (FTP) – an objective way for teachers to improve their work on curriculum planning, student assessment or teaching practice. The literature review 'reveals three common sequences' (p. 35):

presentation	discussion	feedback

The literature also points to two key components of FTP that are essential for its successful implementation:

1. the use of data to inform decisions

2. the collaboration between teachers and administrators in the process.

It is argued that the FTP approach can help teachers become more effective and reflective practitioners. The literature review also highlights the potential benefits for school improvement, such as increased student performance, better communication and improved teacher morale.

Finally, the research highlights some challenges associated with FTP, such as the need for more resources and time and the need for sufficient teacher training in order to ensure successful implementation. It is suggested that more research is needed in this area in order to understand further the effects of FTP on school improvement.

> **To read 'Trust in teacher conversations'**
> **(Man Loon, 2018), scan this QR code**

The tuning protocol

The tuning protocol (fine-tuning a piece of work) is a procedure for structuring a presentation and requesting assistance, reflection, dialogue or feedback about practice. It is believed to have been first developed by the Coalition of Essential Schools in the USA in around the 1990s, and I have also come across the technique under a different name: action learning. There are five main steps, preceded by an introduction. This is followed by a debriefing (to discuss the process). The process can also be used with students during a project, as a formative assessment checkpoint of their work in progress. In this section of the book, I will provide you with an example of using the technique in a leadership scenario within a school or college. Here are the key stages:

Purpose

The tuning protocol is designed specifically because it can be difficult to give feedback diplomatically or hear feedback and not become defensive. It can be used as 'work in progress' or at the end of a piece of work to reflect on results. The purpose is to support an individual with clarification, using critical friendships that are non-judgemental to generate and receive feedback to improve their work. The non-judgemental part is the most difficult.

How to set up

Assemble a small group of four to seven people and arrange them so that they are sitting in a circle with no tables. One person (the presenter) will present a problem. One other person could act as a moderator to quality-assure the principles of the tuning protocol and to keep a sense of timing and etiquette. It is quite easy for one person to upset the process by laughing out loud or not following the correct question procedure.

There are different models available, using different time-frames. This one is particularly useful for teachers who work in the school, because it fits into a ten- to 20-minute window – perfect for people with very little time.

1. Presentation (estimated time three to five minutes)

The presenter – the one sharing a problem publicly – offers one or two key points to be addressed and sufficient information about their issue: how the issue plays on in its context/environment; the situation, time-frame and factors that result in any pros/cons; what they want instead of the problem, etc. The presenter must state as much information as possible that is relevant in order for the participants to be able to understand/respond.

2. Clarifying questions (estimated time five minutes, or longer if the group is larger)

Only include any necessary non-evaluative questions about the presentation, avoiding any suggestion of judgement or advice – for example, closed questions that simply seek clarification and a yes/no response. It is important for the individual to self-regulate their questions or for the moderator to intervene if the question does not seek clarification but evaluation.

Here is a scenario where a teacher (in the stage above) describes why they are having behaviour problems with their class:

The students are not listening, they are talking over each other and they are not paying attention to the teacher's instructions. There is a lack of respect in the classroom, and students are not following the rules or behaving appropriately. The teacher believes that there are several factors contributing to the problem. First, the teacher believes that the same key students are not getting enough SEND (special educational needs and disabilities) support across the school. These students appear to be having problems in other subjects. This may be contributing to the lack of respect in their classroom too. Second, the teacher believes that the students lack motivation. They are not engaged in the lessons, and they are not motivated to put in the effort to learn. The teacher has tried to provide incentives and rewards for good behaviour, but the students are still not responding overall. Third, the teacher believes that the students need more structure and guidance. Now that the teacher has provided an overview, the individuals listening within the tuning protocol pose clarifying questions to understand the problem at a deeper level.

Individual A: 'Do you know what SEND diagnosis your students have?'

(Remember, clarifying questions must be closed and the presenter must reply with a yes or no. If the question is open-ended, the facilitator must ask the individual to rephrase/pose the question. This also ensures that the individuals are fine-tuning their questioning techniques at the same time.)

Presenter: 'Yes.'

Individual B: 'Have you had any support from your head of department?'

Presenter: 'No.'

Individual C: 'Have you raised the problem with your head of department?'

Presenter: 'Yes.'

Individual B: 'What motivation problems do you think your students suffer from?'

Facilitator: *(Interjects)* 'Could you rephrase the question?'

Individual B: 'Have your students shown signs of motivation before?'

Presenter: 'Yes.'

Individual A: 'Do your students show any motivation in each lesson?'

Presenter: 'Yes.'

Individual A: 'Is this motivation sustained by you?'

Presenter: 'Yes.'

Individual C: 'Do you think you should talk with your head of department again?'

Presenter: 'Yes.'

... and so on.

3. Individual writing/assessment (estimated time five minutes)

In silence, each individual writes down their immediate thoughts to generate (wide-ranging) ideas. The individuals cannot ask any other questions and the presenter does not elaborate on any further questions or statements made. The silence ensures that everyone records their immediate thoughts, without one initial comment, question or discussion dictating the conversation, which could result in losing those thoughts or one person dominating the immediate conversation and interrupting everyone else's thought processes.

4. Participant discussion (I like, I wonder...) (estimated time ten minutes)

The presenter remains silent. There are several ways of conducting this stage, but what is most beneficial is that the presenter turns away from the group. This forces them to use their ears only and to hear new solutions or particularly difficult messages they don't want to hear or deal with. An alternative could be that the presenter faces the group but remains silent and avoids eye contact. The presenter is allowed to take notes based on listening to the individuals' discussion. The individuals discuss the issue in the third person. The key message from the critical friendship framework is that the group want to support the individual, so knowing that they cannot see them directly, but know that they are immediately there in the room during the group discussion, develops a process of support rather than adding collateral damage.

For example, 'Why does Ross do this?' or 'How might Ross seek to move forward with X – should he consider doing ABC and abandoning Y and Z?' This is the most significant stage of the tuning protocol for the presenter.

5. Presenter reflection (I have ...) (estimated time three to five minutes)

The presenter now reflects on the group discussion or comments. They can choose to say 'thank you' or elaborate on their thoughts and note-taking as the participants' discussion evolved. The discussion ends and the moderator or group may wish to debrief on the process.

PRACTICAL IDEA

The tuning protocol

I'd like to provide you with two scenarios to explain how you might use the tuning protocol in your classroom with students and also with colleagues.

The classroom scenario

Let's discuss the classroom scenario first. You will need to translate how this will work with your students, whether you teach young children or students on the cusp of higher education. As a teacher, you are facilitating a discussion on the 'cost of living' crisis rippling across Europe in the wake of the Russian–Ukrainian war. How do you set up the process to ensure that all students are participating and that you are acting as a teacher-facilitator, without dominating the discussion but merely facilitating the students' thinking? Of course, there will be some key discussion points that the students will need to consider, with the following established objectives:

- One student (or adult) must facilitate the group so that everyone contributes, whether in speech or in action.

- Another student (or adult) will act as the chair, to be responsible for group behaviour, listening and potential interruptions.

- One student can act as the scribe and another can be nominated to present back to the whole class.

The teacher would like the group to discuss this question:

How can the government support families with the increasing costs of living? Come up with three new policies that the government could implement immediately.

Using the **tuning protocol**, you can set up the discussion in the following way:

1. Begin by asking each student for their opinion on the question. Give each student the opportunity to speak, and everyone must acknowledge each opinion.

2. Ask each student to come up with a policy 'solution' that they think would work.

3. Ask each student to explain their policy idea and also explain why they think it is the best option.

4. Ask the students to discuss the pros and cons of each policy idea.

5. Ask each student to come up with a final policy solution that is a result of their discussion and agreement.

6. Ask the chair to present the final policy solutions to the whole class.

The colleague scenario

Now, let's discuss the colleague scenario. You are a manager in a company and you and your team have been tasked with discussing and coming to an agreement on the best way in which to implement a new method of improving classroom routines to reduce poor behaviour across the school corridors, particularly at the start and end of lesson change-over. Using the tuning protocol, you can set up the discussion in the following way:

1. Begin by asking every team member for their opinion on the question. Give each team member the opportunity to speak, and everyone must acknowledge each opinion.

2. Ask every team member to come up with a policy 'solution' that they think would work.

3. Ask each team member to explain their policy idea and also explain why they think that it is the best option.

4. Ask the team to discuss the pros and cons of each policy idea.

5. Ask every team member to come up with a final policy solution that is a result of the team's discussion and agreement.

6. Ask the team to present the final policy solutions to the whole company.

The process works in the same way, but the level of difficulty and how the process will be conducted will obviously vary between who is taking part, how long they have been allocated and what agreed outcomes are expected.

TOOLKIT TIPS

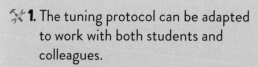**1.** The tuning protocol can be adapted to work with both students and colleagues.

2. Fine-tuning is a diplomatic way in which to give and receive non-judgemental feedback.

3. A moderator or facilitator is **needed** to ensure that students or team members keep to the protocol – this could be the teacher but it doesn't have to be.

4. Everyone should have the opportunity to speak and have their opinion acknowledged.

WORKED EXAMPLE

The tuning protocol can work in these ways:

- It can be used by the teacher to facilitate a discussion.

- Students can facilitate the discussion for themselves, with one student being at the centre of the tuning protocol procedure – if you believe that students can organise the process for themselves. (This will require some training and agreed procedures, and a degree of trust on the teacher's part, to allow the students to complete the process independently.)

Students working independently

1. **Presentation:** A student explains to the group that they want to get the best exam grades they can possibly achieve, but their home circumstances don't allow them to have a quiet space in which to revise. They explain the circumstances and the challenges that they have for staying behind at school to revise and not being late home, and they ask the group how they could resolve this problem before final exams commence in three months.

2. **Clarifying questions:** At this stage, the student presenting this problem now refrain from any further details, and the students who have been listening to the problem pose closed questions that ask the student presenter to respond with a yes or no response. This enables the students who have been listening to ask pertinent questions, but the purpose here is for them to clarify anything that they may have misunderstood or misheard or on which they need further clarity. The art in the process at this stage is the ability to pose the question without having to self-edit as it is being spoken. This is quite a challenge for adults too!

3. **Individual writing:** This stage is tough and it will need some practice before you can allow students to carry it out independently. Students think quietly for themselves, without interrupting each other's thoughts, and write down one or two suggestions that they could then pose to the whole group, while listening to others' suggestions.

4. **Participant discussion:** Once thoughts have been scribed, during this phase the students discuss the pros and cons of each idea. In this stage, the presenting student does not take part in the conversation. Students must be taught how to listen, and in various scenarios you may wish for the presenter to turn away from the group so that they are forced to

listen carefully, which also ensures that the student group are now facing one another, discussing the person in the room. This should instil some trust and reduce fear in those posing difficult questions and challenging ideas, forcing the presenting student to listen carefully to what is being said. With good habits taught, each student should come up with a final solution as a result of their discussion and agree what actions the presenter should take next.

5. **Presenter reflection:** The presenting student would then turn back to the group and be offered an opportunity to reflect on the things that they have heard. The discipline here is that the students who presented some ideas and posed some challenging thoughts remain silent, to allow the presenter to have the concluding remarks. It's an idea that (with training) could work well with Key Stage 4 and 5 students and into higher education.

Students working with teacher facilitation

Are you happy with your finished piece of work or is there something that you still believe that you could do to improve the grade?

This is a question that a teacher could pose to one student in a circle with three or four others. The teacher would leave the facilitation and only intervene when they felt that it was necessary to move the conversation forward. There are several benefits for students. They learn:

- how to listen more effectively

- how to pose more pertinent questions

- where to offer support and where to challenge

- how to critique other group ideas publicly

- how to support somebody else with a familiar or unfamiliar problem

- how to remove bias or preferences and facilitate solutions that suit the individual.

The opening question above would require the presenting student to elaborate on their piece of work, their feelings towards it, the things that they have tried and one or two suggestions for things that they could have done differently as a conversational starter. Following the tuning protocol methodology, the next stage would require students to pose a number of questions to clarify what has been said. The process would then follow the other key stages, using teacher facilitation to the point where students could organise themselves.

The tuning protocol can be used in **small**, public groups in a variety of situations. However, I would be cautious about using this pubic process in any high-stakes scenarios where trust might have already been broken – for example, during capability and disciplinary procedures, school inspections or difficult meetings with parents or colleagues.

TEMPLATE

Tuning protocol

The tuning protocol is a fantastic technique for developing high-performing teams. Try it with a small circle of colleagues first – ensure there is a moderator to guarantee that everybody follows the process and practice with closed tasks before becoming more sophisticated.

Stage	Description	Estimated Time
1	Presentation	3-5 minutes
2	Clarifying questions	5 minutes or longer if the group is larger
3	Reaction	2-3 minutes per person
4	Discussion	10-20 minutes
5	Debriefing	5-10 minutes

CHAPTER 10
WHAT NEXT?

Embedding a questioning culture

In this chapter, we will consider everything that goes on inside a school and how we could use effective classroom questioning strategies to embed a questioning culture in all aspects of school life, from classrooms, to discussions between colleagues, to conversations with parents, governors and the general public. What would we need to do to instil a culture of professional inquisitiveness across the organisation and what methodology should we use for school improvement?

A methodology for school improvement should include the following elements:

1. **Establish a school improvement team:** This could be a team of stakeholders, including administrators, teachers, students, parents and other members of the school community, who work together to identify areas for improvement.

2. **Set goals:** Develop clear and measurable goals to establish the direction for improvement and hold the school improvement team accountable.

3. **Identify priorities:** Identify the most important areas for improvement, based on data and stakeholder input.

4. **Develop an action plan:** Develop an action plan to address the identified priorities, including strategies for implementation, timelines and the resources required.

5. **Monitor progress:** Monitor the progress of the improvement efforts and report back to the school improvement team.

6. **Evaluate outcomes:** Evaluate the impact of the improvement efforts and adjust the action plan as needed.

If we take each of these points above, how could we design a strategy around school improvement, underpinned by effective questioning? I will answer this question in the next section of the book.

EXPLAINER

Imagine if you had already read this book and applied many of the teaching strategies in your classroom, **describe to me** what impact it is having? This is a great example of a miracle question, the technique suggested in this chapter.

Firstly, it's important to unpick the question 'How could we design a strategy around school improvement, underpinned by effective questioning?'

- **Strategy**: We need first to know which people are driving the implementation plan. What is the time-frame available and what are the intended goals?

- **School improvement:** There are many aspects of school that we can improve, such as behaviour, curriculum, reductions in exclusions, increased admissions and parental engagement. I could go on! It is important to define what we want to improve and offer some sensible methods and metrics for success.

- **Effective questioning:** Effective question strategies influence the way in which we work. These need to be defined and translated by teachers working in multiple contexts and by students who will be receiving multiple questions on a daily basis. Some of these strategies may be more beneficial when used with students, others may be beneficial when used with colleagues and, of course, all may be translated and used in other contexts.

Let's consider some effective questioning examples shared so far. Wait time, think, pair, share, cold call and Socratic questioning are all excellent questioning strategies that teachers can use in their classrooms, but they work equally well as a strategy deployed in adult conversations. For example, I may be your line manager and I ask, 'What is it that you are currently struggling with at work?' If I don't offer some take-up time (wait time) for you to process what I've just said, then I am **not** applying the principles that we should use with our students. Perhaps in a teacher training scenario, the think, pair, share method works just as well with colleagues. Using the cold call technique in a teacher training scenario has the potential to become a high-risk strategy. Everybody should be ready to provide an answer, whether it is right or not, and just like we would do in the classroom with students, we need to manage the emotional aspects of learning. Stress, anxiety and non-verbal signals are used to encourage or hinder responses, as well as knowing who to call upon.

Examples from other schools

Now let's address the question: How could we design a strategy around school improvement, underpinned by effective questioning? We could start by looking at the data from high-performing schools for some secrets. For this, we would need to define 'high-performing' so that we can offer reliable solutions. Some definitions could include league tables, numbers of students completing courses, reductions in exclusions and so forth.

In addition, there are thousands of high-performing businesses that have reached national success, such as Just Eat and Uber. What makes these businesses successful? It may well be to do with their leadership teams and their questioning culture. Finally, effective leadership more often than not delivers words of wisdom through effective questioning and active listening.

Effective questioning strategies

Instilling a culture of professional inquisitiveness across an organisation, including classrooms, discussions between colleagues, and conversations with parents, governors and the general public, can be achieved through effective leadership and questioning strategies. Here are some ways to embed a questioning culture in all aspects of school life:

- **Model effective questioning:** The first step to creating a questioning culture is to model effective questioning in the classroom and in all interactions with colleagues, parents and stakeholders. Teachers should ask open-ended questions that encourage critical thinking and reflection, and they should model active listening.

- **Provide professional development on questioning strategies:** Teachers and staff members should be provided with professional development opportunities to learn effective questioning strategies. This can be done through workshops, seminars and online courses.

- **Encourage collaborative learning:** Teachers should encourage students to ask questions and engage in collaborative learning activities that promote inquiry-based learning. This will help to create a culture of curiosity and questioning in the classroom.

- **Foster a safe and supportive environment:** It is important to create a safe and supportive environment where students feel comfortable asking questions without fear of judgement. Teachers should create an atmosphere of mutual respect and trust, where students feel comfortable expressing their ideas and asking for help.

- **Involve parents and stakeholders:** Teachers should involve parents and stakeholders in the questioning process by asking for their input and feedback. This will help to create a collaborative environment that fosters inquiry and exploration.

- **Use technology to enhance questioning:** Technology can be used to enhance questioning by providing access to online resources and tools that promote inquiry-based learning. Teachers can use online discussion boards, interactive quizzes and other digital resources to encourage questioning and critical thinking.

How would I recommend that you use this book and translate some of the ideas into a teacher training session?

The first thing that you need to consider is whether the session will be a one-off or a revisited exercise. Who is the audience? How much do they already know or use? Is the session just to share lots of inspiring ideas (think, pick and mix)? Or are you hoping to introduce one key strategy for all teachers to start using across the organisation?

It is important to remember first and foremost that professional development must be about helping teachers to work better, in order that students can learn and progress. Using research-informed recommendations for teacher professional development, teacher training should be embedded as part of an immersive curriculum for teachers (EEF, 2021). Just like we use retrieval practice techniques with our students, we should deploy the same strategies in our schools for professional development.

To help, I'm going to explain how I would introduce one strategy from inside this book to teachers working in your school. Let's assume that you want to introduce the question matrix (Chapter 7) in a teacher training session in your school. I would first start with sharing the resource in a staff briefing or by email, prior to the actual training event. To ensure that sharing the resource has some impact from a leadership perspective, you may want academic or pastoral leads to spend five minutes talking about the resource with their immediate teams. This will ensure that there are no surprises when all staff come together to be introduced to the technique. Think 'priming' and 'retrieval'.

Let's now consider that you have thought carefully about how you will deploy your colleagues in the teacher training session to work with one another.

This may be paired in teams or mixed with other teachers with whom they would not necessarily work on a day-to-day basis. There are benefits to both models. Remember, teaching is a team sport and no teacher can solve complex classroom problems by themselves. It's important to facilitate the conditions for sharing ideas.

Now, when presenting the idea, we will provide a range of scenarios and examples:

1. in a virtual classroom

2. with Year 2 primary students

3. in a Year 11 English lesson

4. in a teacher training session

5. as a giant poster on display in a classroom

6. as a laminated acetate window to a live display in an art classroom.

Let's consider these six scenarios. Read through the list below and scan the QR codes to watch a video demonstration.

1. **Virtual classroom:** Of course the subject area, the age group, plus the size of the classroom will be a key factor, but I would recommend using the question matrix resource as a discussion prompt. Alternatively, you could activate any online annotation functions and allow students in groups to edit questions for all to see.

2. **Year 2 primary:** Displayed on the board at the front of the classroom, reduce the size of the matrix and add in a relevant image to inspire discussions. Alternatively, teach students how to construct their own questions around your chosen image.

3. **Year 11 English lesson:** For example, each student could have the matrix inside their exercise book and throughout the scheme of work, they can build a series of questions that they could use as revision prompts for building arguments.

4. **Teacher training session:** There are many ways that this can be used across an in-house CPD session. If schools are revisiting policies in order to streamline efficiency and reduce workload, the matrix can be used as a series of questions for group discussions. For example, place the key headlines from your marking policy inside the matrix and discuss how it can be improved using the sentence starters.

5. **A giant poster display:** The matrix framework is printed and placed upon a large space on a classroom wall; a large (replaceable) image is added for each scheme of work. For example, a giant image of Mona Lisa. The image is used to prompt discussions or as a retrieval activity at the start of each lesson. Alternatively, give students sticky notes, ask them to look at the image and then write down a question and place their sticky note in the relevant section on the giant display.

6. **A laminated art periscope:** Cut out the middle area, keeping the left and the top line of the matrix. Tape a layer of acetate to the edges and use the matrix as a periscope/live window of a physical display in the classroom. Alongside students, the teacher looks through the periscope and uses the matrix as a discussion prompt.

PRACTICAL IDEA

Miracle question and clarifying question techniques

There are two questioning techniques that I'd like to share in this section. The **miracle question** evolves from the world of coaching and the **clarifying question technique** from the 'tuning protocol' process, an academic framework for developing critical thinking, where clarifying questions are posed.

The miracle question technique

This is a coaching tool based on solution-focused therapy. A coach asks someone to imagine that overnight a miracle has occurred and their problem has been solved. The coach then asks the client to describe what their world would look like in detail, from the moment that they wake up until the end of the day. This technique helps the client to identify specific goals, which the coach can then help them to work towards in order to solve the original problem.

Imagine that a student is struggling with their behaviour and often finds themselves in trouble. The teacher pulls them to one side and tries to have a rational and calm discussion about the situation, why they are upset and why another person has responded to their frustration. The teacher can then ask the student the miracle question: 'If I could wave a magic wand and **imagine** that this incident didn't happen, **describe to me** how you would feel. How would others respond to you? What do you think the other person would feel?' The student can then start to imagine the potential solutions to their problem and the teacher can help them to break these down into achievable steps that the student can take to move towards a desired outcome. This can be done through setting clear and manageable goals and providing positive reinforcement when the student makes progress. If the student cannot 'imagine' a better solution, this gives the teacher a benchmark from which to rephrase the problem or break down the problem into smaller chunks.

Equally, the technique can be used when working with colleagues. For example, you might be my line manager and in our weekly discussions you discover that I am going through a very challenging workload period and I've lost sense of my deadlines and my personal wellbeing. You can see that it is affecting some of my relationships with colleagues and students in my class. So you pose this question:

'Let's stop worrying about all the deadlines for a moment. Imagine if you tackled the biggest deadline/problem that you have right now. Describe to me what it would be and what positive impact it would have on you managing all the other tasks that lie ahead.'

We can begin to understand how powerful this methodology is to allow the individual to stop, reflect and identify potential solutions. The person posing the miracle question gives the person time to think through possible solutions, with the occasional 'What else?' question to keep pushing the individual for further solutions – within the time-frame available – until all options are exhausted. The questioner should then help to narrow down all the possibilities by asking which options are the best route of action to take. The individual has then identified two or three critical steps that they should take next. Again, just like working with students, if the individual struggles to identify some potential solutions, then we should interene where necessary, offering some suggestions but empowering the individual to make the choice. The crux of this technique is that the questioner replies with 'imagine if' and 'describe to me' as key phrases when repeating back the problem to the other person.

Ultimately, the miracle question technique can be used to provide individuals with a clear vision of the potential solution(s), which helps to break the problem down into achievable steps that are tailored to their needs.

Here are some examples of miracle questions a coach might ask a teacher struggling with a problem, with an 'X' indicating the topic being discussed:

1. If you were to wake up tomorrow and a miracle had occurred, making problem X completely resolved, what would be the first thing you would notice?

2. Imagine you have unlimited resources and support to tackle problem X, what steps would you take to overcome it?

3. If a highly successful teacher who had already overcome problem X were to give you advice, what do you think they would suggest?

4. In an ideal world, what would your classroom look like without problem X, and how would that impact your teaching style?

5. If you could go back in time and give yourself advice before encountering problem X, what would you say?

6. What would it feel like to have completely conquered problem X and how would that change your approach to teaching?

7. Suppose problem X were no longer an issue, what other areas of your teaching would you be able to focus on and improve?

8. If you could borrow the skills or attributes of any teacher who has successfully dealt with problem X, who would you choose and what skills would you borrow?

9. If you had to teach a workshop for other educators on how to overcome problem X, what key takeaways would you want them to learn?

10. Imagine it's a year from now and you've successfully overcome problem X. What steps did you take to get there and what have you learned from the process?

These miracle questions can help the teacher reflect on their situation, identify possible solutions and imagine a future where the problem has been resolved. This shift in perspective can empower the teacher to take proactive steps to address their problem and improve their overall teaching experience. If the teacher cannot imagine a solution, then you can use these miracle questions as a starting point to help them to refine their strategies.

The clarifying question technique

The second technique is used as part of the tuning protocol process. The strategy is to ask pithy questions at the right moment to help to clarify your own understanding of another person's problem. Part of the process is seeking a closed response – a 'yes' or a 'no' ideally – from the other person to help you to understand their context in greater detail.

1. Imagining that their problem has miraculously been solved helps both students and colleagues to see a solution to their problem.

2. Once a solution is identified, break this down into manageable steps that the student or colleague can take towards solving their problem.

3. Ask closed questions to gain greater clarity about a student or colleague's problem.

WORKED EXAMPLE

It's important to **narrow** down the details, unpick any loose terms and generalisations, and seek clarity, depth and detail. For example, let's assume that I am now your line manager and we are talking about a class that you teach, whose behaviour you have struggled to manage. When I ask you for some specific detail, you first respond with:

You: 'It's the boys, they never shut up!'

(I use my clarifying questioning methodology to narrow down the details.)

Me: 'What? All the boys?!'

You: 'No, it's just Freddie and Ahmed.'

Me: 'Really? Freddie and Ahmed never shut up?'

You: 'Well, they do shut up sometimes – when I insist on quiet two or three times or when I teach them on a Monday morning.'

(Having used two clarifying questions, I then choose one area from the above for further clarification.)

Me: 'I've got two further questions. Do you teach Freddie and Ahmed at any other point in the week?'

You: 'Yes, I teach them on Friday afternoon and they are a nightmare.'

Me: 'What are you doing with them on Monday that you're not doing on a Friday?'

To continue with this script, here is the second question:

Me: 'My second question: Imagine if you didn't have to insist on both boys being quiet on two or three occasions. Describe to me a time when you have asked them to be quiet just once and they have responded.'

In the second scenario, I use the clarifying question coupled with the miracle question to seek clarity and help the individual with whom I'm working to at least describe a potential solution.

TEMPLATE

Miracle questions

Use this template as a guide for developing your own miracle questions. Remember, using this strategy is designed to elicit thinking in others, so develop questions carefully, succinctly and with clarity.

Question	Description
1	**What have you tried so far to address the noise in the class?** This question helps the coach understand what strategies the teacher has already employed and what has worked or not worked.
2	**How do you feel when the class is noisy?** This question helps the coach to understand the teacher's emotional response to the noise and how it may be impacting their ability to effectively manage the class.
3	**What do you think the students are trying to communicate through their behaviour?** This question helps the coach and teacher to view the situation from the perspective of the students and to consider what underlying issues may be contributing to the noise.
4	**If the noise in the class disappeared tomorrow, what would be different? How would you feel? What would the students be doing instead?** These questions encourage the teacher to imagine a future without the noise and to explore their desired outcomes.
5	**What are some concrete action steps you could take to move towards your ideal future?** This question helps the teacher generate ideas for addressing the noise in the class and helps to identify specific actions that they can take.

BRINGING IT ALL TOGETHER

What should you do now?

In this final section, I would like to reflect on the ideas shared in the book and discuss what you might do next as a result. I will explain why it is important that you accumulate a range of questioning techniques to a point of automation, to allow you to get on with the day-to-day mechanics of running the classroom, so that you can call upon a range of strategies to respond to the needs of the students as well as holding them to account.

One of my biggest passions is helping teachers to translate academic research into practical techniques for use every day. I have led teacher training in my school career for 25 years and have been running training full time in schools for the last seven or eight years. I will bring together my recommendations for you to consider when planning your teacher training sessions for other colleagues. Context is key! It doesn't matter what strategies you use in the classroom – what matters is **how** you use them. Don't forget to consider the content, age, stage and time of year when implementing them.

This book has offered strategies to help you get started. It is important to use all of them in the right way, considering when, where, how and why they should be used.

If you follow this QR code link, I show you how to put all the strategies together throughout an academic year so that they support and strengthen each other.

And follow this QR code for a video explanation.

Why is effective questioning important?

In the introduction to the book, I estimated the number of questions that a teacher poses on a daily basis in their classrooms and why, using explicit strategies that are embedded as part of our teacher DNA, we can learn to automate some of these techniques. Through routines, teachers can improve effectiveness and reduce workload. The result? We can hold students to account by designing efficient strategies to regularly **'check the learning'** that supports the teaching process more methodically.

The choice to write this book was consciously identified after publishing my last book, *Guide to Memory* (2022). Why? All teachers accumulate curriculum wisdom and develop a range of classroom management strategies to help the teaching and learning process. Through years of experience, teachers learn the **art** of teaching by accumulating thousands and thousands of internal idiosyncratic decisions, each time refining their strategies to improve their effectiveness. Once this is achieved, the classroom – at least on the surface – looks calm and effective and the teacher can start to enjoy their classroom space. For some (although not all), they discover the **science** of teaching, i.e. how we learn so that we can use this information to help make the learning process more efficient, by considering neurodiversity, types of memory and cognitive load. When this blend of art and science comes together, the teacher's experiences and what they now know about cognitive science in the classroom improve many of the techniques that they have used for years, to a point where decisions are made more consciously. These micro-decisions are made, calculated, considered and manipulated to such a degree that nothing is left to chance.

It is my belief that when a teacher has accumulated a wide range of questioning strategies and they know how learning happens, they can then pose a wide range of questions that hook, hold to account, support or hinder, challenge or motivate students at any one moment. This ability to select a suitable questioning strategy and pose questions in such a way as to elicit insightful student responses is nothing short of the work of a genius!

How to use this book for your own and other teachers' professional development

When designing professional development for teachers, it's important to focus on practice that is observable, can be replicated and doesn't degrade the effectiveness of the idea. We know that training that is tailored to the needs of the individual can effectively build knowledge, motivate and develop techniques to improve effectiveness and efficiency. These are immediately weakened the moment that a one-size-fits-all methodology is imposed on all colleagues with the aim of chasing consistency.

All techniques can become effective, but they cannot be applied by everybody at the same time and produce the same result on each occasion. We all like coffee, but we all like to drink it in a different way. How we manipulate the preparation for drinking a cup of coffee is where our wisdom kicks in. Building knowledge takes time, and power from the floor (staff voice) is essential for motivating the workforce and developing techniques. If we want all of the likely outcomes to become changes in practice, this requires regular revisiting and retrieval in order to support staff with embedding ideas.

When translating the ideas in this book into a teacher training session, I recommend the following:

1. Consider how many people will be attending the session. What is their experience? What do they already know? How could you tailor the session to suit different needs?

2. Imagine that you have taught for five hours in the day and then you have to go and sit in a classroom or school hall for one hour to hear somebody else present. How would you like to receive this session? How would you mix up the information to support cognitive load?

3. What content should you revisit to help to strengthen connections to past material?

4. If you shared a short, simple survey, what questions would you ask to help you to prepare for an effective and engaging training session?

5. How is the information going to be presented? Can you share some resources that are dual-coded (images and text)?

6. How will you ensure that all school and college leaders are actively taking part in the training to make sure that there is a collective approach? Think bottom-up and not top-down.

7. How could you get the school/college leadership team to commit to a follow-up session to help to reinforce the material? Think of a future opportunity where colleagues could report back in a 'think, pair, share' or 'show and tell' training session. It doesn't need to be longer than 20 minutes!

8. What examples could you show, particularly in video format, to demonstrate some of the techniques? How could you use some of your own students in some of the material to make it relevant?

9. Could you ask some colleagues to model the technique or provide a range of worked examples/resources?

10. How will you monitor the impact of your training session?

Think about how you would draw up a one-hour teacher training model to be delivered by you after a full teaching day. Here is a potential model:

1. Divide the time available into three 15-minute chunks.

2. Divide the number of people attending into smaller groups.

3. Lead a five-minute opening pitch and a five-minute summary at the end.

4. Provide a number of dedicated spaces where somebody in your organisation will showcase a question strategy, paper-based resource or video clip of a teacher demonstrating the technique with your own students. The number of spaces will be dependent on the number of people attending and the size of the spaces that you have available. I would aim to limit your classrooms to about 15 to 20 people. This makes it small enough for people to have meaningful conversations and for everybody to be heard.

5. At the end of each 15-minute session, your group of teachers should rotate to a new room or the speaker should rotate between rooms.

6. In a follow-up (retrieval) session, teachers should report back after two or three weeks, sharing some of the ideas that they have tried in their classrooms.

It's the simplicity of this model that unlocks powerful teacher training opportunities. Perhaps select one session all teachers must attend, then allow some flexibility – pick and mix choice – to promote professional autonomy.

CONCLUSION
CONTINUING YOUR JOURNEY WITH QUESTIONING

Limitations

As with all teaching books, this book's limitations are in terms of how the ideas are translated, how practical the ideas are in reality, and how a teacher can utilise the strategies with the current challenges of large classes, reduced funding and increasing mental health challenges. Reduced funding and increasing student mental health issues make the jobs of our teachers and school and college leaders very challenging. Access to professional development, online software, courses and teaching materials can make our teachers' work easier. In my years of teaching, there are two challenges that keep returning time and time again. The first? The time needed to help to reinforce the material. The second? The costs associated with professional development, teacher salaries and the funds to secure classroom resources – all of which are significant challenges. Funding in our schools is a political decision, rarely an evidence-based one. We would do well to remember that ALL of our teachers currently working in our classrooms across the UK are nothing short of exceptional! I hope that the ideas in this book make the job more manageable and more fulfilling.

The templates and QR codes threaded throughout this book should enable you to translate the ideas into practice and also disseminate the concepts, research and practical ideas with the colleagues around you. Do let me know your thoughts and share your journey by tagging me in on social media with the hashtag #**GuideToQuestioning**.

Taking it further

For those teachers interested in education research, I thought that it would be worth offering some thoughts from an academic perspective about how you might want to take these ideas forward in some of your own action research in school. Let me start by offering some potential research questions which you may be interested in to inspire your own research, and then I will suggest how you can use this information as part of your performance management appraisal, teacher training sessions or assignments when completing master's degrees or national professional qualifications.

Potential research questions

1. How many different types of question can you pose in one lesson?

2. What is the average 'wait time' delay in your classroom?

3. When posing open/closed questions, how does it impact on student response?

4. What impact does having 'hands down' when a teacher poses a question have on learning?

5. Define learning.

6. What types of question promote study skills?

7. How do questions improve metacognition?

8. What types of question can be used to motivate colleagues?

9. What are the differences between 'think, pair, share' and 'think, pair, share, show me'?

10. What difference do questions that begin with 'how' or 'why' have on learning?

How do I use this in performance management?

A useful methodology to employ might look like this:

1. What do you want to know?

2. What will positive change look like?

3. What is current best practice?

4. How will you collect evidence that is systematic and sustainable?

How do I collect the evidence?

Here are some useful questions to consider to ensure that your research is reliable, robust and ethical.

1. What types of evidence can you gather that will be valid and reliable?

2. What types of evidence should you avoid/disregard?

3. What will be an efficient way of measuring change?

4. What evidence will you produce at the end?

5. What are the pitfalls of evidence collection?

6. How will you collect evidence without it becoming a workload burden?

7. What ethical risks should you consider when collecting the data? For example, student names, photographs, videos, etc.

8. How will you report this information?

9. What tentative claims could you make once you have conducted research?

10. How will you transfer this knowledge from research to teacher development?

If you are seriously considering how to take this book one step further and conduct a research trial in your own classroom, consider the different types of approach that you could use by looking at the table on the opposite page. What research methods will you be using? Remember to factor in the fact that you're likely to be a very busy person if you work within education, and that you need to be realistic with your time!

Will you conduct an experiment, a survey or a case study to document ethnography, with non-participant observation from a distance or participant observation involving direct contact with participants (Gobo, 2008)? When you have considered what approach you will take, you need to consider the technique that you will use to collect your data. This might be in the form of an observation, an interview with teachers or students, a questionnaire, a series of experiments or document analysis. When you have collected your data, you will then need to analyse it and report back. Methods that you could use to do this range from gathering statistics and counting or tallying information, to inputting code or developing a theory or category construction.

Research Framework table

Confirmatory				Exploratory	
Experiment	Survey	Action Research	Grounded Theory	Case Study	Ethnography
Strategies				Methodologies	
True Experiment	Quasi Experiment	Questionnaire	Document Analysis	Interviews	Observations
Variables controlled	'Natural' Experiment	Predetermined (open) response categories	Predetermined analytic (coded) categories	Structured/ unstructured	Structured/ unstructured
Inferential Tests	Descriptive Statistics	Counting/Tally	Coding	Category Construction	Theory Building
Tactics				Techniques	

Adapted from Taber (2013) and Taber (2014).

Whatever you decide to do next, the power of questions – how they are structured and posed – can transform each of our lives. The type of question – how, when and why it is posed – are all important considerations. When we think very consciously about the vast number of questions posed by teachers every day, and even in our everyday lives, we can understand that questions are used to garner more information as a human. As a time-limited teacher, working with a large number of people at once, you need to be extremely efficient and effective in your methods in order to make the classroom a highly productive place. Having the ability to do this sets you apart from the general population.

Just as I started this book with an opening question, I'll finish with a closing question: 'Now that you have read this book, what you are going to do?'

Further reading

Here is a list of sources that have inspired my journey to understanding the science behind questioning. If you want to take your learning further, I heartily recommend you take the time to delve into these publications yourself.

Open thinking, closed questioning: Two kinds of open and closed question, by Peter Worley

Mary Budd Rowe: What a Researcher Can Say to Science Teachers, by Julie A. Bianchini and Nicole I. Holthuis

Questions for research-informed performance management

Questions for school governors

School leadership interview questions

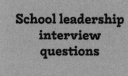

Teaching interview questions and templates

Fermi Questions

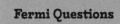

Watch Ross showcase Staffordshire University Academy's questioning approach to performance appraisal

How learning happens

REFERENCES

Anderson, L. W. and Krathwohl, D. R. (eds) (2001), *A Taxonomy for Learning, Teaching, and Assessing: A revision of Bloom's taxonomy of educational objectives*. New York: Addison Wesley Longman.

Appleby, J. (1998), *Becoming Critical Friends: Reflections of an NSRF Coach*. Providence, RI: The Annenberg Institute for School Reform at Brown University.

Arnold, M. (2020), 'Giving students a chance to learn: Hitting pause and engaging students', *Journal on Empowering Teaching Excellence*, 4, (2), article 3.

Bambino, D. (2002), 'Redesigning professional development: Critical friends', *Educational Leadership*, 59, (6), 25–7.

Bianchi, L., Whittaker, C. and Poole, A. (2021), 'The 10 key issues with children's learning in primary science in England', University of Manchester and The Ogden Trust, www.scienceacrossthecity.co.uk/wp-content/uploads/2021/03/3634_Childrens_Learning_in_Primary_Science_Report_2020_v8.pdf

Bianchini, J. A. (2008), 'Mary Budd Rowe: A storyteller of science', *Cultural Studies of Science Education*, 3, 799–810.

Bloom, B. S. (1956), *Taxonomy of Educational Objectives, Handbook: The Cognitive Domain*. New York: David McKay.

Breslin, T. (2021), *Lessons from Lockdown: The Educational Legacy of COVID-19*. Abingdon: Routledge.

Breslin, T. (2023), 'Schooling during lockdown: Experiences, legacies, and implications', in J. M. Ryan (ed) *Pandemic Pedagogies: Teaching and Learning During the Covid Pandemic*. Abingdon: Routledge, Chapter 6.

Buchanan-Hill, J. (2016), 'Questioning techniques: A study of instructional practice', *Peabody Journal of Education*, 91, (5), 660–71.

Choi, I., Land, S. M. and Turgeon, A. G. (2005), 'Scaffolding peer-questioning strategies to facilitate metacognition during online small group discussion', *Instructional Science*, 33, (5), 483–511.

Coe, R. (1998) 'Can feedback improve teaching? A review of the social science literature with a view to identifying the conditions under which giving feedback to teachers will result in improved performance', Research Papers in Education, 13(1), pp. 43–66.

Coe, R., Rauch, C. J., Kime, S. and Singleton, D. (2020), 'Great Teaching Toolkit: Evidence review', Evidence Based Education, https://2366135.fs1.hubspotusercontent-na1.net/hubfs/2366135/Great%20Teaching%20Toolkit%20Evidence%20Review.pdf

Collins, B., Day, R., Hamilton, J., Legris, K., Mawdsley, H. and Walsh, T. (2020), '12 tips for pivoting to teaching in a virtual environment', [version 1]. *MedEdPublish* 2020, 9:170

Cushman, K. (1998), 'How friends can be critical as schools make essential changes', *The Coalition of Essential Schools*, 14, (5), 1–8.

Dalim, S. F., Ishak, A. S. and Hamzah, L. M. (2022), 'Promoting students' critical thinking through Socratic method: Views and challenges', *Asian Journal of University Education*, 18, (4), 1034–47.

Department for Transport (2021) Reported road casualties Great Britain: e-Scooter factsheet 2021, GOV.UK. Available at: https://www.gov.uk/government/statistics/reported-road-casualties-great-britain-e-scooter-factsheet-2021/reported-road-casualties-great-britain-e-scooter-factsheet-2021

Dillon, J. T. (1985), 'Using questions to foil discussion', *Teaching and Teacher Education*, 1, (2), 109–21.

CONCLUSION

Ding, N., Xu, X. and Lewis, E. (2022), 'Short instructional videos for the Tiktok Generation', *Journal of Education for Business*, pp. 1–11. Available at: https://doi.org/10.1080/08832323.2022.2103489.

Donohoo, J., O'Leary, T. and Hattie, J. (2020), 'The design and validation of the enabling conditions for collective teacher efficacy scale (EC-CTES)', *Journal of Professional Capital and Community*, 5, (2), 147–66.

Dulfer, N., Kriewaldt, J. and McKernan, A. (2021), 'Using collaborative action research to enhance differentiated instruction', *International Journal of Inclusive Education*, DOI: 10.1080/13603116.2021.1992678.

Dunlosky, J. et al. (2013), 'Improving students' learning with effective learning techniques', *Psychological Science in the Public Interest*, 14(1), 4–58.

Education Endowment Foundation (EEF) (2020), 'Remote learning: Rapid evidence assessment', https://educationendowmentfoundation.org.uk/public/files/Remote_Learning_Rapid_Evidence_Assessment.pdf

Education Endowment Foundation (EEF) (2021), 'Effective professional development: Guidance report', https://educationendowmentfoundation.org.uk/education-evidence/guidance-reports/effective-professional-development

Ellis, K. (1993), 'Teacher questioning behavior and student learning: What research says to teachers', paper presented at the 64th Annual Meeting of the Western States Communication Association, Albuquerque, NM, 12–16 February 1993, https://files.eric.ed.gov/fulltext/ED359572.pdf

Feely, M. and Karlin, B. (2022), *The Teaching and Learning Playbook: Examples of Excellence in Teaching*. Abingdon: Routledge.

Forrester, T., Sandison, C. E. and Denny, S. (2017), 'A secondary mathematics teacher's perceptions of her initial attempts at utilising whiteboarding in her classes', in A. Downton, S. Livy and J. Hall (eds), *40 Years On: We Are Still Learning*. Melbourne: MERGA, pp. 1–8.

Gobo, G. (2008), *Doing Ethnography*. London: SAGE Publications.

Hammond, Z. (2020), 'The power of protocols for equity', *Educational Leadership*, 77, (7), 45–50.

Hargreaves, A. and Fullan, M. (2012), *Professional Capital: Transforming Teaching in Every School*. New York: Teachers College Press.

Ilgen, D. R., Fisher, C. D. and Taylor, M. S. (1979), 'Consequences of individual feedback on behavior in organizations', *Journal of Applied Psychology*, 64, (4), 349–71.

Investors in People (IIP) (no date), 'St Petrocs & Investors in People: Our story', www.investorsinpeople.com/community-stories/iip-st-petrocs-our-story

Izzati, T. G. and Wahyuni, D. S. (2021), 'Teacher's questioning in classroom interaction towards students' learning process in an EFL classroom', *English Education Journal*, 9, (3), 279.

Judd, C. H. (1914), 'Some observations in German schools', *The Elementary School Teacher*, 14, (9), 437–44.

Knowles, M. S. (1984). *Andragogy in Action: Applying Modern Principles of Adult Learning*. New York: Wiley.

Lemov, D. (2010), *Teach Like a Champion*. Hoboken, NJ: Jossey-Bass.

Levin, T. and Long, R. (1981), *Effective Instruction*. Washington DC: ASCD.

Man Loon, M. (2018), 'Trust in teacher conversations: A case study of using a fine tuning protocol in an international school', Ed.D. thesis, Education University of Hong Kong.

Matsumoto, D., Hwang, H. C. and Sandoval, V. (2015), 'The funnel approach to questioning and eliciting information', *Tactics and Preparedness*, 15, 7–10.

Mayer, R. E. (1999), *The Promise of Educational Psychology: Vol. 1, Learning in the Content Areas*. Upper Saddle River, NJ: Prentice Hall.

Mayer, R. E. (2002), *The Promise of Educational Psychology: Vol. 2, Teaching for Meaningful Learning*. Upper Saddle River, NJ: Prentice Hall.

Mayer, R. E. and Moreno, R. (2003), 'Nine ways to reduce cognitive load in multimedia learning', *Educational Psychologist*, 38, (1), 43–52.

McGill, R. M. (2017), *Mark. Plan. Teach*. London: Bloomsbury Education.

McGill, R. M. (2022), *The Teacher Toolkit Guide to Memory*. London: Bloomsbury Education.

Moir, T. (2018), 'Why is implementation science important for intervention design and evaluation within educational settings?', *Frontiers in Education*, 3, article 61.

Ofsted (2023), 'Finding the optimum: The science subject report', www.gov.uk/government/publications/subject-report-series-science/finding-the-optimum-the-science-subject-report--2

Paivio, A. (1986), *Mental Representations: A Dual Coding Approach*. Oxford: Oxford University Press.

Paul, R. and Elder, L. (2006), *Critical Thinking: Learn the Tools the Best Thinkers Use*. New Jersey: Pearson Prentice Hall.

Quinn, M. and McGill, R. (2019), 'UCL verbal feedback project report', University College London, https://discovery.ucl.ac.uk/id/eprint/10111936/1/2019_verbal_feedback_project_final_4_print.pdf

Ren, X., Tong, Y., Peng, P. and Wang, T. (2020), 'Critical thinking predicts academic performance beyond general cognitive ability: Evidence from adults and children', *Intelligence*, 82, 101487.

Rice, G. T. (2018), *Hitting Pause: 65 lecture breaks to refresh and reinforce learning*. Virginia: Stylus Publishing.

Robinson, C., Gallus, J., Lee, M. and Rogers, T. (2018, 'The demotivating effect (and unintended message) of awards', SSRN Electronic Journal [Preprint], https://doi.org/10.2139/ssrn.3219502

Rolls, L. and Hargreaves, E. (2022), 'Enabling parity of participation by listening to "pupil voice"', in J. Biddulph, L. Rolls and J. Flutter (eds), *Unleashing Children's Voices in New Democratic Primary Education*. London: Routledge, Chapter 3.

Rotter, J. B. (1966), 'Generalized expectancies for internal versus external control of reinforcement', *Psychological Monographs: General and Applied*, 80, (1), 1–28.

Rowe, M. B. (1974), 'Wait-time and rewards as instructional variables: Their influence on language, logic, and fate control', *Journal of Research in Science Teaching*, 11, (2), 81–94.

Rowe, M.B. (1986),'Wait time: Slowing down may be a way of speeding up!', Journal of Teacher Education, 37(1), 43–50.

Sandling, J. (2021), 'EEAA questioning technique for teachers [ask better questions]', https://jonathansandling.com/humix/video/20e54758d3e9c8dbd12311e7f2ea0a70fbb640da16ae7d57ed42c8f4bbb8d306

Shernoff, D. J., Csikszentmihalyi, M., Shneider, B. and Shernoff, E. S. (2003), 'Student engagement in high school classrooms from the perspective of flow theory', *School Psychology Quarterly*, 18, (2), 158–76.

Skene, K., O'Farrelly, C. M., Byrne, E. M., Kirby, N., Stevens, E. and Ramchandani, P. G. (2022), 'Can guidance during play enhance children's learning and development in educational contexts? A systematic review and meta-analysis', *Child Development*, 93, (4), 1162–80.

Stevens, R. (19 12), *The Question as a Measure of Efficiency in Instruction: A Critical Study of Class-Room Practice*. New York: Teachers College, Columbia University.

Storey, V. A. and Wang, V. C. X. (2016), 'Critical friends protocol: Andragogy and learning in a graduate classroom', *Adult Learning*, 28, (3), 107–14.

REFERENCES

Swaffield, S. (2008), 'Critical friendship, dialogue and learning, in the context of leadership for learning', *School Leadership & Management*, 28, (4), 323–36.

Sweller, J. (1988) 'Cognitive load during problem solving: Effects on learning', *Cognitive Science*, 12(2), 257–285.

Sweller, J., Van Merriënboer, J. J. G. and Paas, F. (1998), 'Cognitive architecture and instructional design', *Educational Psychology Review*, 10, 251–95.

Taber, K. S. (2013). *Classroom-based Research and Evidence-based Practice: An introduction* (2nd ed.). London: Sage

Taber, K. S. (2014) *Methodological issues in science education research: a perspective from the philosophy of science. In M. R. Matthews (Ed.), International Handbook of Research in History, Philosophy and Science Teaching* (Vol. 3).

Thulasidas, M. and Gunawan, A. (2022), 'Cold calls to enhance class participation and student engagement', Proceedings of the 2022 IEEE International Conference on Teaching, Assessment, and Learning for Engineering, Hong Kong, 4–7 December 2022, https://ink.library.smu.edu.sg/cgi/viewcontent.cgi?article=8556&context=sis_research

Tienken, C. H., Goldberg, S. and Dirocco, D. (2009), 'Questioning the questions', *Kappa Delta Pi Record*, 46, (1), 39–43.

Tierney, S. (2016), *Liminal Leadership: Building Bridges across the Chaos... Because we are Standing on the Edge.* Woodbridge: John Catt Educational.

Tomlinson, C. A. (2001), *How to Differentiate Instruction in Mixed-Ability Classrooms* (2nd edn), https://rutamaestra.santillana.com.co/wp-content/uploads/2020/01/Classrooms-2nd-Edition-By-Carol-Ann-Tomlinson.pdf

Weisberg, D., Hirsh-Pasek, K., & Golinkoff, R. (2013). *Guided play: Where curricular goal meet a playful pedagogy. Mind, Brain, and Education*, 7, 104– 112.

Wilen, W. W. (1991), *Questioning Skills, for Teachers: What Research says to the Teacher* (3rd edn). Washington DC: National Education Association.

Williamson, R. A. (1996), 'Self-questioning – an aid to metacognition', *Reading Horizons: A Journal of Literacy and Language Arts*, 37, (1), article 3.

Worley, P. (2015), 'Open thinking, closed questioning: Two kinds of open and closed question', *Journal of Philosophy in Schools*, 2, (2), 17–29.

INDEX

DOWNLOADABLE TEMPLATES

Template: Pose, pause, pounce, bounce

Template: Wait time

Template: Mini whiteboards

Template: Convergent questions

Template: Cold calling

Template: Gadfly, midwife, stingray, uninformed

Template: MALI

Template: Funnel questions

Template: ABC

Template: Question matrix

Template: EEAA

Template: Tuning protocol

Template: Miracle questions

ABOUT THE AUTHOR

Ross is known globally as @TeacherToolkit. To date, over 19 million people have read his website! He began teaching in 1991 and taught design and technology for 26 years in some of London's most challenging secondary schools; 20 years as a school leader. In 2015, he was nominated as one of the '500 Most Influential People in Britain' by *The Sunday Times* and remains the only classroom teacher to feature to this day. Today, he works with students, teachers and school leaders worldwide, enhancing teaching and learning, workload and teacher mental health.

As one of the most followed educators globally on social media, Ross offers unique social media insights and support for teachers, schools and organisations. He is frequently asked to speak at national conferences and has worked with over 100,000 teachers worldwide. He is regularly asked to reflect on educational developments in multiple publications about education policy, championing the brilliance of teaching and unpacking the complexity of the classroom. Ross is also a PGCE tutor and visiting tutor at the University of Buckingham and when not struggling with his doctoral research, he is either teaching teachers, creating resources or tweeting @TeacherToolkit! Ross is the bestselling author of *Mark. Plan. Teach. 2.0* , *Teacher Toolkit*, *Just Great Teaching* and *The Teacher Toolkit Guide to Memory*.

Total number of questions in the book:
ANSWER = 378